THE STEAM LOCOMOTIVE SHED

• BRITAIN'S LIFE AND TIMES •

THE STEAM LOCOMOTIVE SHED

A third illustrated tribute

Photographs from the Ray Ruffell Collection

Selected and described by
John Stretton

• RAILWAY HERITAGE •
from
The NOSTALGIA *Collection*

Photographs from the Ray Ruffell Collection © Silver Link Publishing Ltd; other photographers as individually credited
Text © John Stretton 2003

First published in 2003

British Library Cataloguing in Publication Data

A catalogue record for this book is available from the British Library.

ISBN 1 85794 174 8

Silver Link Publishing Ltd
The Trundle
Ringstead Road
Great Addington
Kettering
Northants NN14 4BW

Tel/Fax: 01536 330588
email: sales@nostalgiacollection.com
Website: www.nostalgiacollection.com

Printed and bound in Great Britain

All photographs are by Ray Ruffell unless otherwise credited.

A Silver Link book
from
The NOSTALGIA *Collection*

Frontispiece A visit to a steam shed was full of promise, often presenting varied and interesting scenarios. On 3 December 1965, at Guildford, No 76053 is temporarily 'hors de combat', hoist for a running repair by the steam crane, flanked by Nos 31405 (left) and 33027, somewhat impatiently awaiting coal. Sadly, the latter's impatience was not to last long, withdrawal coming on 10 January 1966, less than two months after transfer to Guildford.

ACKNOWLEDGEMENTS

As explained in the Introduction, this book has been put together around a selection from the Ray Ruffell Collection. The final product has been a collaboration between many people, but initial gratitude and thanks, for her courtesy, co-operation and sheer warmth and humanity, must go to Ray's widow Joan. It is she who had the foresight to ensure that this extensive collection was not split, and she is to be congratulated. After Joan must come Peter Townsend at Silver Link Publishing, who had the vision for the project and the confidence to see it through. I hope and trust that neither he, Joan nor you, the reader, will be disappointed. I have enjoyed the challenge, and among others involved who deserve thanks are: Hugh Ballantyne, John Edgington (for both his wealth of knowledge and proof-reading), Mike Esau (for his expertise in the darkroom), Bob Essery (again for help behind the scenes and for proof-reading), Peter Fitton, Tom Heavyside, Mark Hoofe, David Johnson at Millbrook House Ltd, and Brian Morrison. In addition, the following publications have been invaluable: Michael McManus's *Ultimate Allocations* (listing all allocations of steam, diesel and electric locomotives between 1948 and 1968!), Chris Banks's *British Railways Locomotives 1948*, and the two excellent volumes of *The Directory of British Engine Sheds*, produced by Roger Griffiths and Paul Smith. Finally, my wife Judi has been as accommodating, encouraging and patient as ever – often at no small cost and frustration to herself! To you all, I say a big 'Thank you'.

CONTENTS

A classic locomotive portrait and one displaying two aspects of the appeal of shed visits. The first was the opportunity to see engines resting between duties or standing idle, often from attractive vantage points, presenting great opportunities for even the amateur photographer. Here the camera has been used with skill as, on an unknown date but probably in the late 1950s, No 30453 *King Arthur* exemplifies the attraction, especially in its pristine (ex-Works?) condition, as it prepares for its next duty at Reading (South) shed. The first of the Maunsell-variant 'King Arthurs' to enter traffic, from Eastleigh in February 1925, *Arthur* went to his round (turn)table in the sky on 23 August 1961. The second appealing aspect? What was a Salisbury loco doing here? *Ray Ruffell Collection*

INTRODUCTION

The first two volumes in this series – by David Hucknall and Roger Siviter respectively – were by and large an exploration of the compilers' own photographs, supplemented by an array of other photographers' material. This latest largely turns this philosophy on its head, featuring the collection of a third party seasoned by guest appearances. Other than the front cover, there are none of my own photographs included herein; the closest I get is including material from my collection of prints accumulated over many years. Obviously I would have wished to 'show off' my own work, but there was, quite simply, just too much superb material demanding inclusion in the limited available space.

The 'featured artist' in these pages is Ray Ruffell, and the book is readily dedicated to him and his work. He was only a shadowy published figure compared to the likes of Dick Riley, Ivo Peters, Eric Treacy, Brian Morrison, Gavin Morrison (no relation), Ken Fairey, W. A. C. Smith, Hugh Ballantyne, Alec Swain, etc, etc, but he was a prolific and talented cameraman and, as an employee of the railways, was able on occasion to go 'where others feared to tread'! Having had access to Ray's collection after his untimely death in November 1998, I have been astounded at the breadth of his railway interest, both in this country and abroad. I doubt that there was much generically that escaped his lens! He obviously enjoyed visiting loco sheds and it is with very great pleasure that I have selected some of the mountain of prints for this book. As usual, the heartache is knowing what to leave out, but I hope and trust that the reader will accept my choices and share my enjoyment of his images and those of the other contributors.

As for the layout, I have mixed and matched, hopefully to present a varied and appetising menu, juxtaposing 'spread shot' and 'sharp focus'. Taking any form of classification into consideration, an author immediately becomes a hostage to fortune. Readers will note on the Contents page chapters entitled 'Small...', '...medium...' and '...large'; the criteria for these may be a little arbitrary on my part and I beg forgiveness if choices clash with others' perceived boundaries. For the purposes of this volume, 'small' indicates an allocation of fewer than 50 locomotives, 'medium' is 50-99, and 'large' anything thereafter. This has led me to some surprising re-arrangements, after initial choices based on my own (unscientific) preconceptions – for example Grantham, which I have always considered to have been at least a medium shed, amazed me at only having an allocation of 35. This is, of course, the danger of viewing an installation from its size and apparent importance, rather than the actual work required of it.

Actual allocation figures are from my own records and relate to my calculations of distribution as at 31 August 1950. A full list of 343 coded depots is given on pages 9-11, but it may be of interest to the reader to learn that there were 183 sheds with allocations of fewer than 50, 110 between 50 and 99, and 50 above that figure. Stratford was the largest with 383, and there were just two others in excess of 200 – St Margaret's, Edinburgh, and New England,

Peterborough. All of these are allocations allotted to the main shed code and may include any locomotives at sub-sheds; indeed, the eagle-eyed may spot some in the 'small' section that would appear to be in the wrong part of the book. The reasoning here is that the sheds thus depicted were in themselves small and would, undoubtedly, if they had an 'official' allocation at all, have been smaller than the magic 50 figure. Again, I beg indulgence if this offends! The directions to one or two sheds are reproduced from the December 1947 edition of *The British Locomotive Shed Directory*, compiled by R. S. Grimsley.

My own baptism into shed worship came at Leicester (Midland) in my early teens, when steam still very much ruled supreme. I have been a lover of the genre ever since, even into the desert days of diesels and electrics. The preparation of this book has been an unmitigated joy for me – unmitigated, that is, apart from the burden of having to wield the scalpel to some photographs that deserved entry but were brutally excluded solely due to that lack of available space. They are being kept in reserve for Volume 4, which will feature yet another prolific but largely unsung photographer and which is already in early preparation!

THE STEAM LOCOMOTIVE SHED

LOCOMOTIVE SHED ALLOCATIONS AS AT 31 AUGUST 1950

Code	Shed name	Allocation	Code	Shed name	Allocation	Code	Shed name	Allocation
1A	Willesden	135	9D	Buxton	55	19C	Canklow	54
1B	Camden	56	9E	Trafford Park	72	20A	Leeds (Holbeck)	96
1C	Watford	30	9F	Heaton Mersey	63	20B	Stourton	48
1D	Devons Road (Bow)	48	9G	Northwich	42	20C	Royston	61
2A	Rugby	98	10A	Springs Branch (Wigan)	57	20D	Normanton	48
2B	Nuneaton	73	10B	Preston	36	20E	Manningham	45
2C	Warwick	16	10C	Patricroft	73	21A	Saltley	180
2D	Coventry	12	10D	Plodder Lane	17	21B	Bournville	30
3A	Bescot	67	10E	Sutton Oak	39	21C	Bromsgrove	10
3B	Bushbury	41	10F	Wigan (CLC)	12	21D	Stratford-upon-Avon	13
3C	Walsall	57	11A	Carnforth	42	22A	Bristol (Barrow Road)	56
3D	Aston	53	11B	Barrow-in-Furness	50	22B	Gloucester	
3E	Monument Lane	33	11C	Oxenholme	8		(Barnwood)	43
4A	Bletchley	60	11D	Tebay	10	23A	Skipton	36
4B	Northampton	40	12A	Carlisle (Upperby)	87	23B	Hellifield	23
5A	Crewe North	85	12B	Carlisle (Canal)	58	23C	Lancaster	41
5B	Crewe South	103	12C	Penrith	6	24A	Accrington	29
5C	Stafford	23	12D	Workington	27	24B	Rose Grove	50
5D	Stoke	99	12E	Moor Row	12	24C	Lostock Hall	43
5E	Alsager	18	14A	Cricklewood	89	24D	Lower Darwen	37
5F	Uttoxeter	6	14B	Kentish Town	116	25A	Wakefield	123
6A	Chester	38	14C	St Albans	17	25B	Huddersfield	41
6B	Mold Junction	39	15A	Wellingborough	74	25C	Goole	34
6C	Birkenhead	93	15B	Kettering	38	25D	Mirfield	40
6D	Chester Northgate	9	15C	Leicester (Midland)	80	25E	Sowerby Bridge	33
6E	Wrexham	29	15D	Bedford	42	25F	Low Moor	37
6F	Bidston	8	16A	Nottingham	143	25G	Farnley Junction	50
7A	Llandudno Junction	31	16B	Kirkby-in-Ashfield	62	26A	Newton Heath	167
7B	Bangor	33	16C	Mansfield	29	26B	Agecroft	56
7C	Holyhead	23	17A	Derby	136	26C	Bolton	47
7D	Rhyl	27	17B	Burton-on-Trent	110	26D	Bury	28
8A	Edge Hill	112	17C	Coalville	32	26E	Bacup	11
8B	Warrington	59	17D	Rowsley	52	26F	Lees (Oldham)	25
8C	Speke Junction	49	18A	Toton	156	26G	Belle Vue	31
8D	Widnes	26	18B	Westhouses	61	27A	Bank Hall	46
8E	Brunswick	36	18C	Hasland	49	27B	Aintree	55
9A	Longsight	129	18D	Staveley	71	27C	Southport	29
9B	Stockport Edgeley	27	19A	Sheffield (Midland)	81	27D	Wigan (Central)	42
9C	Macclesfield	11	19B	Millhouses	41	27E	Walton-on-the-Hill	20

Code	Shed name	Allocation	Code	Shed name	Allocation	Code	Shed name	Allocation
28A	Blackpool	61	50A	York	176	64C	Edinburgh	
28B	Fleetwood	33	50B	Leeds (Neville Hill)	81		(Dalry Road)	46
30A	Stratford	383	50C	Selby	60	64D	Carstairs	50
30B	Hertford East	0	50D	Starbeck	45	64E	Polmont	43
30C	Bishops Stortford	0	50E	Scarborough	13	64F	Bathgate	38
30D	Southend (Victoria)	0	50F	Malton	16	64G	Hawick	24
30E	Colchester	67	50G	Whitby	13	65A	Eastfield	164
30F	Parkeston	30	51A	Darlington	117	65B	St Rollox	77
31A	Cambridge	99	51B	Newport	108	65C	Parkhead	68
31B	March	161	51C	West Hartlepool	77	65D	Dawsholm	43
31C	Kings Lynn	47	51D	Middlesborough	64	65E	Kipps	53
31D	South Lynn	34	51E	Stockton	54	65F	Grangemouth	36
31E	Bury St Edmunds	14	51F	West Auckland	40	65G	Yoker	11
32A	Norwich	130	51G	Haverton Hill	21	65H	Helensburgh	6
32B	Ipswich	91	51H	Kirkby Stephen	11	65I	Balloch	4
32C	Lowestoft	37	51J	Northallerton	13	66A	Polmadie	167
32D	Yarmouth		51K	Saltburn	11	66B	Motherwell	115
	(South Town)	22	52A	Gateshead	89	66C	Hamilton	51
32E	Yarmouth (Vauxhall)	0	52B	Heaton	119	66D	Greenock	42
32F	Yarmouth (Beach)	17	52C	Blaydon	79	67A	Corkerhill	91
32G	Melton Constable	25	52D	Tweedmouth	47	67B	Hurlford	56
33A	Plaistow	83	52E	Percy Main	24	67C	Ayr	59
33B	Tilbury	21	52F	North Blyth	44	67D	Ardrossan	35
33C	Shoeburyness	37	53A	Hull (Dairycoates)	144	68A	Carlisle (Kingmoor)	141
34A	Kings Cross	160	53B	Hull		68B	Dumfries	38
34B	Hornsey	81		(Botanic Gardens)	50	68C	Stranraer	13
34C	Hatfield	28	53C	Hull (Springhead)	54	68D	Beattock	12
34D	Hitchin	33	53D	Bridlington	10	70A	Nine Elms	100
34E	Neasden	81	53E	Cudworth	6	70B	Feltham	77
35A	New England	213	54A	Sunderland	58	70C	Guildford	57
35B	Grantham	35	54B	Tyne Dock	48	70D	Basingstoke	22
35C	Peterborough (Spital)	43	54C	Borough Gardens	47	70E	Reading (South)	18
36A	Doncaster	182	54D	Consett	13	71A	Eastleigh	145
36B	Mexborough	120	60A	Inverness	58	71B	Bournemouth	52
36C	Frodingham	70	60B	Aviemore	7	71C	Dorchester	14
36D	Barnsley	40	60C	Helmsdale	5	71D	Fratton	49
36E	Retford	64	60D	Wick	5	71E	Newport (IoW)	15
37A	Ardsley	88	60E	Forres	6	71F	Ryde (IoW)	12
37B	Leeds (Copley Hill)	39	61A	Kittybrewster	70	71G	Bath (Green Park)	51
37C	Bradford	49	61B	Aberdeen (Ferryhill)	40	71H	Templecombe	23
38A	Colwick	199	61C	Keith	24	71I	Southampton Docks	16
38B	Annesley	76	62A	Thornton Junction	112	72A	Exmouth Junction	122
38C	Leicester (Central)	23	62B	Dundee (Tay Bridge)	101	72B	Salisbury	57
38D	Staveley (GC)	34	62C	Dunfermline (Upper)	75	72C	Yeovil (Town)	15
38E	Woodford Halse	53	63A	Perth	138	72D	Plymouth (Friary)	23
39A	Gorton	161	63B	Stirling	49	72E	Barnstaple Junction	13
39B	Sheffield (Darnall)	95	63C	Forfar	21	72F	Wadebridge	5
40A	Lincoln	64	63D	Fort William	12	73A	Stewarts Lane	112
40B	Immingham	120	63E	Oban	7	73B	Bricklayers Arms	140
40C	Louth	11	64A	Edinburgh		73C	Hither Green	51
40D	Tuxford	15		(St Margaret's)	220	73D	Gillingham	38
40E	Langwith Junction	61	64B	Edinburgh		73E	Faversham	31
40F	Boston	49		(Haymarket)	79	74A	Ashford	63

Code	Shed name	Allocation	Code	Shed name	Allocation	Code	Shed name	Allocation
74B	Ramsgate	43	83C	Exeter	35	86E	Severn Tunnel Junction	74
74C	Dover	68	83D	Plymouth (Laira)	108	86F	Tondu	48
74D	Tonbridge	61	83E	St Blazey	32	86G	Pontypool Road	89
74E	St Leonards	29	83F	Truro	23	86H	Aberbeeg	38
75A	Brighton	73	83G	Penzance	30	86J	Aberdare	52
75B	Redhill	30	84A	Wolverhampton		86K	Abergavenny	37
75C	Norwood Junction	39		(Stafford Road)	66	87A	Neath	57
75D	Horsham	25	84B	Oxley	67	87B	Duffryn Yard	
75E	Three Bridges	31	84C	Banbury	70		(Port Talbot)	54
75F	Tunbridge Wells	24	84D	Leamington Spa	32	87C	Danygraig	34
75G	Eastbourne	33	84E	Tyseley	118	87D	Swansea East Dock	30
81A	Old Oak Common	197	84F	Stourbridge Junction	88	87E	Landore	65
81B	Slough	48	84G	Shrewsbury	122	87F	Llanelly	85
81C	Southall	73	84H	Wellington (Salop)	24	87G	Carmarthen	45
81D	Reading	95	84J	Croes Newydd	51	87H	Neyland	45
81E	Didcot	47	84K	Chester	57	87J	Goodwick (Fishguard)	14
81F	Oxford	56	85A	Worcester	87	87K	Swansea (Victoria)	48
82A	Bristol (Bath Road)	100	85B	Gloucester		88A	Cardiff (Cathays)	80
82B	Bristol			(Horton Road)	101	88B	Cardiff (East Dock)	62
	(St Philips Marsh)	145	85C	Hereford	53	88C	Barry	80
82C	Swindon	127	85D	Kidderminster	19	88D	Merthyr	55
82D	Westbury	74	86A	Newport		88E	Abercynon	27
82E	Yeovil (Pen Mill)	10		(Ebbw Junction)	143	88F	Treherbert	40
82F	Weymouth	32	86B	Newport (Pill)	57	89A	Oswestry	55
83A	Newton Abbot	73	86C	Cardiff (Canton)	106	89B	Brecon	11
83B	Taunton	58	86D	Llantrisant	20	89C	Machynlleth	56

One of Ray Ruffell's delights was travelling by train – on or off duty! – and many trips were made for pleasure, and passed steam sheds en route. On 24 August 1962, during a ride on that day's 'Pines Express', he passed Templecombe (Somerset & Dorset Joint) shed (71H), which was host to No 2219, while an unidentified ex-S&D 2-8-0 rested at the side of the building. Originally timber as constructed by the S&DJR in 1863, it had passed its use-by date by the time of nationalisation and was replaced in 1951 by a standard BR brick and concrete edifice, topped off with an asbestos roof across a steel frame. Closure, with the S&D system, came in 1966, but the structure, in commercial occupation, still stood three decades on. The train locomotive is not recorded, but appears to be a Standard Class 5 4-6-0.

In September and October 1961, Ray Ruffell made visits to the depots of South Wales. On 22 September one of the stops was at Rhymney, where No 5681 was photographed standing parked in the afternoon sunshine on a short siding with brake-van attached, while residing inside the shed were 'sisters' Nos 5660 and 5655.

Built in 1864, originally with a pitched slate roof, the three-road shed survived to see its centenary, but closed a year later in March 1965. Note the wooden signal box squeezed between the buffer stop and shed wall.

THE STEAM LOCOMOTIVE SHED

1.
SMALL...

The trip on 7 October was largely by rail, restricting wide access, but Ray still managed to include several of the smaller installations. Again blessed with sunshine, he snapped Merthyr's depot from the train, where he recorded that 'there were six panniers in and around the shed'. Sadly, the number of the loco nearest the camera is not recorded, but using a glass it appears to be in the 96XX series; another pokes out of the shed entrance and two more are 'hiding' on the far side of the rake of coal wagons. Opened in 1853, this was the third site for a shed in Merthyr. Improvements were made both to the shed itself and coal stage (right) over the years, with the depot finally closing on 2 November 1964 and the building let out to industrial use; it was finally demolished during the early 1990s.

Dowlais (Cae Harris) came after Merthyr, and this time a ground visit was managed. No 5610 is seen taking water, while fellow class members Nos 5681 (seen at Rhymney opposite) and 5662 take temporary respite inside the shed building. One of three depots in the Dowlais area, Cae Harris opened in 1876, adjacent to the station. It closed as a steam shed in December 1964, but stayed open as a diesel stabling point for a little over a decade.

Above Diminutive tanks were often associated with small sheds, and the ex-GWR '14XX' auto-tanks were widespread in their work and distribution. On 16 October 1961 No 1466 undertakes some light shunting in the shed yard at Tiverton Junction on a bright autumn day, while the small shed building itself, to the left, stands empty. This one-road shed, with coal stage and water column by the entrance, was opened in 1932, replacing the ex-Bristol & Exeter facility constructed on adjacent land in 1848. No 1466 was withdrawn from Taunton shed on 28 December 1963, but happily found salvation in preservation at Didcot Railway Centre.

Below By contrast, small shed and large loco! Seemingly built to just accommodate the railway's loading gauge, Barnstaple shed's entrance is barely high enough to permit entry to 'Battle of Britain' No 34064 *Fighter Command*, photographed on the same day as the view above. Barnstaple had three separate stations and as many shed sites, although evidence of some of the sites is inconclusive. The wooden two-road shed seen here is that adjacent to Junction station, opened in 1863 and closing 101 years later in September 1964. Allocated to Salisbury at the date of this photograph, *Fighter Command* saw trips to Nine Elms and Eastleigh, before finally settling back at Salisbury eight months prior to withdrawal on 27 June 1966.

Right Horsham was in the heart of a web of lines radiating (broadly) north, west, east and south in LB&SCR country, with a first shed opening as early as 1848. The later edifice, slightly to the north and across the tracks, appeared in 1896, originally with ten roads but enlarged in 1901 by a further eight. On 9 November 1961 ex-LB&SCR 0-6-2T 'E4 Radial' No 32470 stands by the low-level coaling stage line with the end wall of the 1901 extension in the background. Officially closed to steam on 18 July 1959, locos still visited and were stabled thereafter, as shown by the Three Bridges 'E4' seen here. The loco was withdrawn (from Brighton) eight months later, and the shed was demolished in 1969.

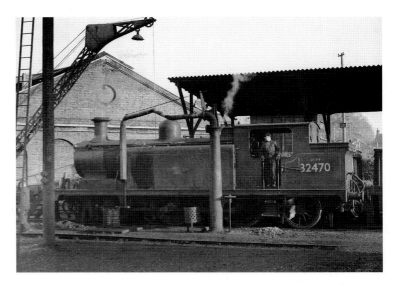

Below Wellington, Shropshire, shed was one of the GWR's northerly outposts, hosting a variety of visiting motive power not necessarily reflecting its actual allocation. Situated on the north side of the station, the three-road shed opened in 1876 and was probably a conversion from an existing goods shed. The end came just a year after this view, on 10 August 1964. No 9774 moved to Tyseley with the closure of the shed, but on 19 August 1963 stands ready for its bunker to be replenished, while Nos 41232 and 9630 stand in the yard. The driver, carrying a bag under his arm, walks purposefully across the tracks – on his way home?

SMALL...

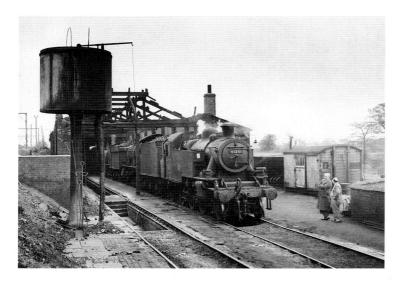

Top A product of GWR/LNWR collaboration, Crewe (Gresty Lane) was truly a small shed, originally seeing the light of day in 1870. Shoehorned between electrified lines (on the extreme left) and open fields, the two-road building, doubled in length in 1913, had room for a handful of visitors and covered accommodation for even fewer. Over the years, however, even this latter facility was denied locos and crews alike, as can be seen on 12 May 1963, as the foreman engages in conversation, perhaps explaining what happened to the roof or discussing closure, which came on 17 June. Catering for locos working into Crewe via Wellington and Market Drayton, MR and GWR types wait their chance to return 'home'. No 41201 of Wellington heads the row, which also contains Nos 6903 *Belmont Hall* and 6821 *Leaton Grange*. *Peter Fitton*

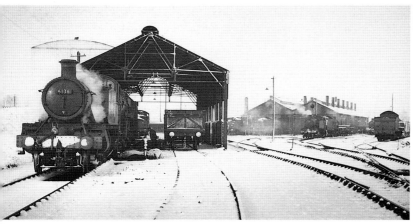

Middle A shed with, perhaps, a surprisingly small allocation was Didcot. At the junction of two important GWR main lines and with its own local work, one might be forgiven for expecting a greater allocation (in 1950) than 47 locomotives. A railway life is often romanticised, but the operations were no joke during hard winter weather. On just such a day, 13 January 1964, No 6136 stands wreathed in steam, a small oasis of warmth in the cold and bleak shed yard scene. The 1932-vintage shed and most of the locos outside are covered in snow; a 'Standard' hides behind No 6136 in the rudimentary shelter, the attention of a no doubt very cold railwayman.

Bottom The diminutive shed facilities at Exmouth were relatively rarely photographed, but on 12 May 1964 Ray visited, and, from the station platform, captured No 41206 being prepared for a return run up the branch. This SR concrete structure replaced the original Exeter & Exmouth Railway timber version in 1927, and its felt and tar pitched roof was replaced by corrugated asbestos around the time of nationalisation. The end had come on 8 November 1963, with the site being swallowed by a new road scheme some time later. No 41206 fared slightly better, lasting until 27 March 1966, then a resident of Templecombe.

THE STEAM LOCOMOTIVE SHED

Above Basingstoke was another shed that I would not have thought would fall into the 'small' category, but its allocation of just 22 in 1950 belied its importance as a facility serving both main-line and cross-country routes. The last of three depot sites at Basingstoke, this three-road facility opened in 1905 on the north side of the line, west of the station. Although officially closed by BR in March 1963, Ray records there being 18 engines on shed on 12 July 1964, including No 31835, seen here in company with Nos 34040 *Crewkerne*, 73110 *The Red Knight* (with the large BR1F tender), 30830 and 33023.

Below Two years later, on 5 September 1966, the shed is still in use as a stabling point, seen this time from the other side of the main line, as No 34013 *Okehampton* accelerates away from Basingstoke station with its rake of Pullman coaches forming the down 'Bournemouth Belle'. The end finally came in July 1967, with the end of steam on the Southern Region, and demolition followed two years later. *Okehampton* also survived to the end, being withdrawn from Salisbury after the last day on 9 July 1967 and cut up at Cashmore's, Newport, in November, after appearing at Bristol (Bath Road)'s Open Day the previous month.

SMALL...   17

Above Weymouth shed was photographed from the 3.50pm train to Waterloo in the watery late afternoon sunshine of 3 February 1965. In the yard, at the south end of the shed, Bulleid 'Pacifics' stand cheek-by-jowl with ex-LMS 2-6-2T No 41298 and a 'Hymek' diesel. Once more the importance of the location, the terminus of both a commuter and holidaymaker branch, outweighed the purely local work operated by this three-road shed of GWR origins and known locally as 'Radipole'. Opened on this site in 1885, it closed as a steam shed, like Basingstoke, on 9 July 1967, but remained open until 1970 for the stabling and servicing of diesels; it was demolished in 1971. Note the ex-GWR water tank and repair shop to the left of the main shed building.

Below Branksome, on the western outskirts of Bournemouth, was truly a small facility. Of S&DJR origin and serving the southern end of that railway, the two-road shed stood in the triangle of lines from the town's station to both Bournemouth West and Central. Opened by the S&D in 1895, it was closed by the LMS as a wartime economy measure, but resurrected after the hostilities. Final closure came on 2 August 1965, less than five months after this view on 10 March, as No 41243 passes with a four-coach Templecombe-Bournemouth West S&D line train.

THE STEAM LOCOMOTIVE SHED

At the other end of the country, another shed at the side of the main line was Tebay. Its importance was largely the provision of 'bankers' to assist trains up Shap. Originally a LNWR depot (in 1861), in 1947 it was completely replaced by the LMS (as a four-rather than five-road shed) on the same site south-west of the station. BR installed a new coaling plant and 60-foot turntable as late as 1956, but this only gave limited service as the shed was closed on 1 January 1968 and demolished within months. On 19 June 1965, photographed from the 9.25am Crewe-Perth express, No 42225 and a sister engine wait their turn for this work, while two railwaymen discuss some vital subject. An East London engine at nationalisation (allocated to Plaistow), No 42225 arrived at Tebay three months prior to this shot and lasted until 16 July 1966.

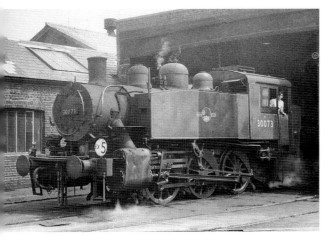

Southampton Docks Shed was another location that did not enjoy many published photographs, inevitable, perhaps, due to its location, raison d'être and unglamorous nature. Exclusively occupied by tank locomotives, again because of the nature of the work, the 'USA' tanks were long-time residents. The site had originally been utilised by stables, which had been converted to a one-road shed by the Southampton Docks Company in 1865; this was replaced by a two-road structure in February 1879. In the 1930s a third road was added and the roof extended, but BR reconstructed all of this in 1955. Closed to steam in 1963, it continued to provide shelter until the end of steam on the SR in July 1967, before being finally demolished in the late 1970s. On 20 July 1965 what looks to be a fellow enthusiast peers from the cab of No 30073 as it stands proudly wearing its 'EX5' duty disc at the entrance to the shed.

Another location and another 'USA'. This time the resident is not in capital stock, but became part of the ex-SR Departmental fleet in October 1962 after the dieselisation of Southampton Docks. DS233 (formerly No 30061) is temporarily out of work on 24 July 1965, taking advantage of a rest in the mouth of the quite literally 'small shed' at Redbridge Sleeper Depot. A stone, dead-end 'garden shed', with pitched slate roof, it sat on the south side of the Southampton-Bournemouth line at Redbridge. Closure to steam came in 1967, but it remained in occasional use by diesel shunters until the end of the 1980s.

Special tours and trips – preferably by rail – were a great favourite with Ray, where he mixed with both enthusiasts and fellow railwaymen. On 5 March 1966 he was a member of the LCGB's 'Somerset & Dorset Railtour', and part of the itinerary included Highbridge, where the train engine took water. No 41307 is seen having its thirst slaked in the bright afternoon sunshine, watched intently by an admiring crowd. The two-road shed, seen in the background, was part of the ex-S&DJR Works complex on the site and opened, together with the Works, in 1862. Formal closure of the shed was on 11 May 1959 (the Works had died in 1930) but, as can be seen, basic services were still available for locos working into Highbridge.

THE STEAM LOCOMOTIVE SHED

Above The Isle of Wight was a delightful place in steam days, with little tanks scurrying around the island like something out of 'Thomas the Tank Engine'. In latter days the sole remaining shed was at Ryde, itself the last of three separate such facilities in the town. Totally new in 1930, at the end of the yard to the west of the station, it was of steel frame construction, with concrete block infilling and a corrugated asbestos transverse pitched roof. On 11 September 1965, a little over a year before closure, the collection of locos resting between duties in the late summer sunshine includes (left to right) Nos 26 *Whitwell*, 27 *Merstone*, unidentified, 35 *Freshwater*, and 22 *Brading*. All survived until the latter days of steam on the island, but only No 24 *Calbourne* escaped into preservation. *Hugh Ballantyne*

Below Equally delightful was (and still is) the Vale of Rheidol Railway, inherited by British Railways from the GWR in 1948. What appears to be a two-road shed is, in fact, a legacy of two separate corrugated iron buildings being constructed by the VofR in 1902! By the time of this view, on 13 July 1966, the two had been joined, with No 7 *Owain Glyndwr* awaiting replenishment with coal and water outside the longer of the two sheds. Closed in 1968, when trains and locos were diverted to the main-line station and ex-BR shed in the town, this site was fairly quickly cleared.

SMALL...

These three views show long-abandoned sheds. In the first, despite appearances, Ascot loco shed, photographed on 25 June 1969, is not 'active' and is not long for this world. Built by the L&SWR in 1889 to replace the existing facilities on the opposite side of Ascot station, and abandoned as home to any locos since as early as 1937, the wooden structure was not suited to modern operations and was demolished just two months after this view was taken.

Nine months later, on 19 March 1970, another depot has 'ceased to be'. Once a LB&SCR facility, Leatherhead opened on 8 August 1859 but closed as early as 1874, being converted soon after into private use. As seen here it is in use as a garage by Ryebrook Motors – home to rubber rather than steel! Previous devotions had been as a chapel and school – a small one at that! Final demolition came in the late 1980s.

The rails are still there, but not in current use, in this view of Ash loco shed on 17 June 1970. Initially a two-road affair, one being devoted to locos and one to goods, in 1905, courtesy of a L&SWR/SER joint effort, it was completely remodelled to the one-road structure seen here. Although closed by the SR in 1946, loco use continued into BR days, before it was finally converted into private use.

THE STEAM LOCOMOTIVE SHED

Above Tewkesbury shed was a magnificently small affair, tucked away from the station and running line – a modeller's dream! To local crews it was known as Tewkesbury 'loco' and, although a couple of miles away, on the MR branch to Great Malvern, it acted as the servicing point for motive power on trains terminating at Ashchurch, on the Birmingham-Bristol main line. Thus, once more, its size belied its operating importance. The remains of a water column can be seen, and a small lean-to has replaced a pitched extension to the Malthouse of earlier times. On 12 August 1961 the depot is home to two 'rivals' – ex-LMS No 43754 and ex-GWR No 7788. Closure came one year later on 7 September 1962. *David Johnson*

Below Equally small, but this time in full view of the travelling public, was Brimscombe shed, on the 'Golden Valley' Gloucester-Swindon route. The extension, crowned by a water tank, is clearly visible, providing a cavernous entrance to the shed building. The main need here was for banking to Sapperton Tunnel, the job being handled on 7 March 1964 by No 4109, almost six months after the official closure of the shed by BR. Allocated to Gloucester (Horton Road) since 1961, No 4109 did not last much longer after this visit to Brimscombe, being withdrawn on 4 May 1964. *Hugh Ballantyne*

2.
READING SOUTH

Allocation in 1950: 18. Closed: 6 April 1964 (officially January 1965).

READING.
The shed is on the north side of the line east of the station. The yard is visible from the line. · It is also visible from the main G.W. line.

Turn left outside the main entrance to the G.W. Station, and bear left past the entrance to the S.R. Station. Continue along Blagrave Road (parallel to the S.R. line). Turn left into Vastern Road under the S.R. bridge. The shed entrance is a gate on the right hand side before the G.W. over-bridge. Walking time 5 minutes.

Ray Ruffell's first posting on the railway was as a cleaner at Reading South depot in 1952, where he not only enjoyed his time and the work, but also spent many hours with his camera, recording the day-to-day events and operations. This section shows some of those recordings.

Like many other enthusiasts, he enjoyed the loco portrait. In an early such 'record', 'U' Class No 31631 is seen 'fed and watered' and ready to work its next diagram southwards on 11 June 1957. Introduced by Maunsell in March 1931, this Ashford-built tender version of the ill-fated 'River' Class 'K' 2-6-4Ts was the second of the final batch of Class 'U' locos to enter service and was initially without smoke deflectors. In common with its last-batch 'sisters', it was also provided with a larger, 4,000-gallon tender with a turned-in top, as seen here, rather than the type gracing the earlier class members. Allocated to Guildford – hence the 70C shedplate – since May 1954, it finally succumbed to the inevitable on 14 October 1963.

Above Despite its small allocation, the ex-Southern Railway facility at Reading was important in a way similar to Weymouth and other 'terminal' depots. At the end of a long branch, both engines and crews sought routine care and attention, together with the occasional more serious remedial work required. On 10 July 1959 the shed yard is well stocked with locos waiting their turns, including Nos 31807, 31616, 31864 and 31412. Note the Southern signal box in the background, guarding the SR main line and entry to both station and shed.

Below Another loco portrait, this time of a design from an older generation. Ex-SE&CR 'C' Class No 31723 looks in fine condition as it stands ready to return south on 6 February 1960. Ray records that he had worked this loco into Reading the previous day, on a freight from Guildford in company with driver M. Hockley, and it would seem that he had a soft spot for it! Perhaps it also pleased its masters, as it only had two depots during BR days – Bricklayers Arms at nationalisation until 17 December 1956, then Guildford until withdrawal on 1 February 1962. A good and faithful servant.

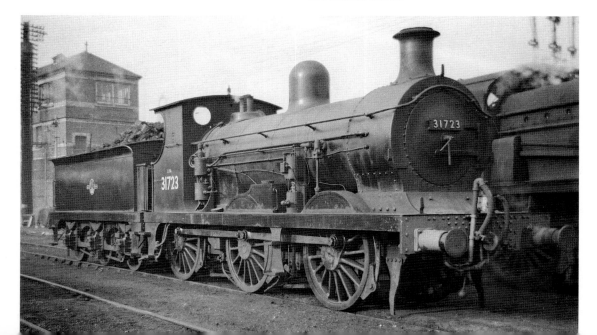

Above The shed at Reading was sandwiched between two Regions' running lines on the final approach to the town. The ex-GWR main line out of Paddington is seen on the low embankment beyond the shed, while the SR line into Reading South station runs behind the photographer. Seen from the gantry that carried the Advanced Starter signal, on 8 February 1960, the shed has a typical look of a Sunday – locos scattered everywhere, crammed into every available free space. Left to right, we see Nos 33007, 73085, 31852, 31830, 31867, and, to add some glamour, 'Schools' No 30903 *Charterhouse*. In the mid-1950s the gable ends to the shed were rebuilt and the roof re-clad in corrugated asbestos sheeting; however, here the former looks to have seen many summers of engine exhaust! Note the proximity to the GWR station in the left background.

Left This could almost be the ground view of that above, but it is a different day. On Tuesday 17 February 1960 we see a comparison of front ends between 'S15s' Nos 30836, anxious to be going, and 30847, and 'H15' No 30489. While the two 'S15s' (new in December 1927 and December 1936 respectively) both survived until 1964, No 30489, one of Urie's originals from 1914, went under, from Nine Elms, on 10 February 1961. Happily, No 30847 survived its 'holiday' at Barry Docks to be preserved on the Bluebell Railway.

THE STEAM LOCOMOTIVE SHED

Right Ray captioned this shot 'Steam's Finest Hour'. Perhaps somewhat debatable, it certainly captures steam activity on two different Regions. Taken from the footplate of No 31826 and looking across its untidy and dubious-quality tender coal on 16 February 1960, No 30540 is in the shed yard in the foreground, while No 30837 climbs the bank between the SR and WR with the 9.00am freight from Guildford to the Western Region. In the distance an unidentified 'Castle' blasts its way out of Reading General station with an up express bound for Paddington.

Below Opposite we saw the view of the shed looking towards the west; this is the easterly aspect, seen on 17 February 1960. Taken from the Starter signal on Platform 1 of the Southern station, the cramped conditions are well shown, with goods stock having to find space alongside the locomotives in the tight strip of land between the two Regions' running lines (GWR to the left and SR to the right, out of the picture). Several brake-vans congregate in the foreground, while in the distance, just visible through the lowering steam and the haze of the early morning wintry sunshine, are Reading's gasholders.

READING SOUTH

Below Like most sheds, there were occasions when 'foreigners' would visit. Some were unannounced and/or unwelcome, but neither applies to this duo of GWR 0-4-2Ts on 19 April 1960. Supposedly en route to Swindon from Weymouth, Nos 1474 and 1453 proudly pose, with WR driver Taylor taking the opportunity to have his portrait recorded too. Having been at Weymouth since 1958, No 1474 was officially transferred to the WR earlier in April 1960 and was due to be added to Reading (GW)'s books on the 23rd of the month, but here appears to wear an 82A Bristol (Bath Road) shedplate! No 1453 was destined for Slough (records again show the 23rd), having been a resident of Weymouth since nationalisation; perhaps both were running to Swindon for a 'once-over', having been in 'Southern' hands!

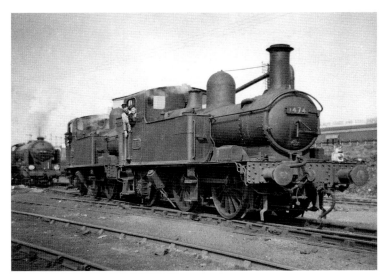

Bottom 'Schools' were regular visitors to Reading South, with services over the Redhill-Reading route. No 30906 *Sherborne* was glimpsed behind the two 14XX tanks above, and is seen here on shed again on 10 May 1960, receiving replenishment by hand from 'coalman' Bob Hill before moving to the station to head the 3.35pm service to Redhill. Officially transferred to Guildford two months before this view, the loco still wears the previous 70A (Nine Elms) shedplate. It was briefly transferred to 75A (Brighton) on 19 November 1962, from where it was withdrawn on 1 January 1963, in common with all the other then extant members of the 'Schools' Class. Note the towering ex-GWR East Main signal box in the background.

THE STEAM LOCOMOTIVE SHED

Above For the photographer, sheds gave ample opportunities for artistic and/or aesthetic shots. Ray was no stranger to these, and his 'eye' is demonstrated by these two views from 4 March 1964. In the first, under leaden skies, No 80140 stands impatiently waiting to be turned, with the fireman assessing the situation, after working a passenger turn from Redhill into Reading South station, while on the left No 33009 hogs the turntable road, taking a drink after working a freight from Feltham. To the right, No 31790 is more patiently waiting for its call to head a passenger train to Guildford.

Below Rather than focusing on the locomotive, Ray has here framed an unidentified 2-6-4T between the two buffer stops at the end of the track at the back of the shed. The end in other ways was not far off, the shed officially closing just a month later on 6 April.

Above Just nine days after the previous views, the end is shown in yet another way. Dieselisation, well under way on the Southern Region, is exemplified here as the shape of things to come (certainly in the short term) with D6505 like a cuckoo in the nest on 13 March. To the right, Nos 75077 and 31413 are not giving up without a fight, although the latter lasted only until 22 June, withdrawn from Guildford. New on 6 May 1960 from Birmingham Railway Carriage & Wagon Co, and allocated to Hither Green, D6505 moved to Eastleigh on 27 August 1962 – its depot in this view. Renumbered 33005 under BR's 'TOPS' scheme in February 1974, it served that same depot until withdrawal on 25 June 1987.

Above right Having moved across the yard and on to the GW 'old bank' embankment carrying the link between the SR and GWR metals, Ray presents an alternative view of No 75077 on the same day, but this time in company with No 31869. Though healthily in steam here, the end came for this 'N' within six months, on 17 August. Note the visiting SNCF wagons in the left and centre foreground.

Right Five months after the shed closed, although it had to all intents and purposes only been a stabling point for some time, the yard is temporary home to a rare visitor. Seen on 24 September 1964, No 45346 has been turned and is ready to make its way back to the Midlands, having worked into the South station at the head of the 11.20am ex-Redhill passenger, courtesy of a WR 2-6-0 that had failed due to a tender hot box. Allocated to the ex-GC shed at Annesley at this date, a move to Lostock Hall came on 3 June 1965, followed by brief residences at Trafford Park and Stockport (Edgeley) before withdrawal on 15 July 1967.

THE STEAM LOCOMOTIVE SHED

Above The months are lengthening since closure, and although visiting locomotives are still housed, the run-down of the facility is gathering momentum, judging by the ad hoc termination of a former yard through road with a makeshift stop block and warning light! In the sunshine of 21 August 1965 No 31866 waits to return to Redhill, while an unidentified Type 3 diesel hides within. No 31866 became a casualty of the progressive elimination of steam on the SR, falling foul of 'HQ's pen' on 10 January 1966. It had been a Guildford loco for eight days short of a year.

Below Eight days later and a 'Tadpole' DEMU passes the shed on the final approaches to the Southern station with another service from Redhill. The progressive abandonment of the shed site is obvious. Weeds are everywhere, ash and clinker lay discarded where thrown from locos, and just one diesel rests inside the shed building; cars are even parked on previous trackbed space at the western end of the shed.

Above Compare this view with the upper one on page 31. The date is now 27 November 1965 and the wreckers have obviously moved in! The damp weather does nothing to lift the sense of desolation and wanton abandonment. The refurbishment of the building a decade earlier seems a world away and was certainly not to prove economic!

Below A fortnight on and, viewed from the coal road, there is obviously no hope of a reprieve. On 11 December brick, concrete, wood and twisted metal lay strewn, with smoke drifting from smouldering embers of already burnt timbers. The ex-GWR main line can be seen to the right – nowadays, looking at the site from a Paddington train, it is hard to imagine/realise that the Southern Railway/Region ever existed here. Such is progress!

3.
...MEDIUM...

Below Both alphabetically and romantically, Bath (Green Park) stakes great claim for the opening spot in this section. At the northern end of the route from Bournemouth, it was an automatic Mecca for enthusiasts from the Midlands and the North keen to sample the delights of the Somerset & Dorset line. Reflecting the variety of motive power on the services, a visit to the shed was an equal feast of old and new, small and large. On 24 August 1962, as a passenger on the 'Pines Express', Ray captured this delightful panoramic view of the shed yard, displaying the 1935-redesigned layout. To the left No 73054 stands aloof from the rest, which are standing outside the original S&DJR 1874 and 1878 extension timber sheds and include an ex-S&DJR 2-8-0 and 'Standard' Class 3 2-6-2T. The stone building to the right is the first shed on the site, built by the MR in 1869.

Right In an earlier time, the ex-MR shed building, seen on the right of the previous view at Bath, hosts the meeting of ex-LMS locos from north and south. On Saturday 15 May 1955, No 40509 (left) has reached the spa town on a train from Templecombe and proudly wears that depot's code. Two days later, however, it was officially transferred to Bath, so this sighting could have been the transfer move. By contrast, its companion, No 44333 of Saltley shed, has worked a service down from the Midlands. It had been a Saltley engine since 1951 and remained so until 9 December 1961, when it moved eastwards to Coalville. *Hugh Ballantyne*

Below right On 5 March 1966 Ray again visited Bath, as one of a party of enthusiasts (including young children and at least one babe in arms!). Using the signal box as a

THE STEAM LOCOMOTIVE SHED

vantage point, Bath MR's shed building is seen again. With the opening of the S&DJR facilities, this building became a predominantly repairs facility, but here looks to be out of use, with a grounded coach body parked at the entrance. The loco numbers are not recorded, but No 80043 can be identified (left) as possibly the only locomotive in steam.

New to Bletchley in August 1952, it became a Southern animal from December 1959 and served at various depots until its final journey to Templecombe in 1964. That shed closed two days after this shot – with the closure of the S&D route – and No 80043 succumbed to its fate 20 days later, a mere stripling at less than 14 years old.

Another town that has always been a magnet for tourists, but one that is very different from Bath in its attractions, is Blackpool. There were both similarities and distinct differences in railway operations between the two, one of the latter being displayed here on Central shed on 28 September 1964. Having been cleaned by the photographer and his friend Paul Claxton, 'Royal Scot' No 46160 *Queen Victoria's Rifleman* of Carlisle (Kingmoor) takes pride of place in the yard, displaying an unconventional positioning of its '1X37' coding and ready for a return working to Glasgow. Keeping it company, left to right, are station pilot No 47468 and 'Black Fives' Nos 44900 and 45067. Originally a four-road shed built by the Blackpool & Lytham Railway in 1863, the L&YR replaced it with an eight-road successor with a northlight-pattern roof in 1885. This, in turn, was re-roofed in 1957 with the steel and glass roofing seen here. Formal closure came less than two months after this shot, on 2 November 1964, but the facility remained in place for a period thereafter to accommodate visiting locomotives. Demolition came later, the site becoming a car park. *Peter Fitton*

THE STEAM LOCOMOTIVE SHED

Above There are many places in the UK that owe their growth and popularity to the coming of the railway. Among these, and certainly high up on the list, is Bournemouth. A mere hamlet until late Victorian times, its population explosion was dramatic once branch lines reached the area from east, then west, in 1870 and 1874. The shed that lasted until the end of steam on the SR was not the first. Constructed in 1888 (at a cost of £6,419) to be the main facility for what became known as Central station (but only housing eight locomotives under cover), it was extended at the rear (out of sight here to the left) in 1937, and was then rebuilt with a taller entrance and steel and corrugated asbestos sheeting in 1953. That work is seen here on 4 March of that year, with No 30548 just glimpsed inside and not much work evident on the ground! *MJS collection*

Below Seen from the signal box, the shed yard, across the running lines from the station (out of sight to the right), is not unduly active on 10 September 1966, with Nos 80085, 34024 *Tamar Valley* and 76011 taking things easy. All three survived to be withdrawn in July 1967, at the demise of steam on the SR.

Above Two years earlier than the previous view, business is certainly much brisker. The cramped layout of the yard and the need to carefully plan loco positioning are well evidenced here on 26 July 1964 as No 34046 *Braunton* receives coal from one of the yard cranes. To the right, No 34085 *501 Squadron* heads a line of 'Standards', including No 76012. With an allocation of 52 in 1950, the shed and yard foremen had to be masters of their task! Despite looking the part, *Braunton* and *501 Squadron*, both Bournemouth engines since 1959 and 1961 respectively, were not to survive much longer, the end for both coming on 25 October 1965. No 76012 was withdrawn from Guildford in September 1966.

Above right On 24 February 1968 snow can be seen on the background hillsides and the sky looks ominously full of more. Buxton is renowned for being no stranger to snowflakes ('If it snows anywhere, it snows in Buxton!') and men and locos had to be ready for anything that was thrown at them. By the nature of the work demanded of them, engines stabled here were gutsy and workaday – no temperamental or lightweight examples were tolerated. One week before closure, steam still holds sway, largely in the form of Stanier's '8Fs', but Class 40 and 25 diesels occupy the 'luxury' of the roofless shed.

Right On the same day, two of the '8Fs' stand by the shed building. Swindon-built No 48471, complete with mini-snowplough, simmers quietly over the pit, waiting for its next duty, while No 48424 appears to be already cold, having worked its last; it was withdrawn almost literally as Ray took this shot. Its companion was slightly more successful, soldiering on until 18 May 1968. A Buxton incumbent at the time of this view, it had previously worked on the WR and only returned to the LMR, at Newton Heath, on 28 May 1966; its final move, concurrent with the closure of Buxton shed at the beginning of March, was to Heaton Mersey. Note on the right the ex-LNWR Southern Division four-wheel tender, here converted as a mobile water tank for the Cromford & High Peak line.

THE STEAM LOCOMOTIVE SHED

Above Another slightly surprising shed was Leeds (Holbeck). As an outside observer, I would have thought it a 'large' shed under our criteria, but on the basis of allocations – 96 in 1950 – it falls (just) within the 'medium' category. That said, it housed a wonderful pot pourri of locomotive types and ages throughout its life, reflecting both the importance of its Anglo-Scottish express work and the nature of its more local needs. The extensive shed, constructed by the MR in 1868, replaced earlier facilities; it finally closed its doors just seven months from its centenary, on 2 October 1967. On 26 April 1958 No 41196 (of 24J) stands in company with a relative newcomer, No 73011. Although outwardly in fine condition, No 41196, a Lancaster (Green Ayre) loco since March 1952, had only weeks left, being withdrawn on 12 July 1958. *J. K. Morton, MJS collection*

Left For those of us living south of Leeds, the 'Standard' 'Clans' were both intriguing and elusive. While visits to the city were not rare, they were, nevertheless, not common. On 8 September 1963 No 72007 *Clan Mackintosh* makes a fine sight at Holbeck as it receives careful attention from its crew prior to returning to (presumably) Carlisle over the S&C line. The 'Clans' never received the adulation from crews or enthusiasts lavished on the 'Brits', and the first five (Scottish-allocated) were summarily withdrawn on 19 January 1963, after only 11 years of service. A Carlisle (Kingmoor) loco for the whole of its life, No 72007 entered service on 19 April 1952 and 'retired' on 4 December 1965. *MJS collection*

THE STEAM LOCOMOTIVE SHED

Above Machynlleth was a 'no-go area' for many, being situated in the wilds of West Wales on the long cross-country route from Shrewsbury to Aberystwyth/Pwllheli. Ever the preserve of small engines, it had a surprisingly large allocation in 1950 of 56, belying its location and the size of the shed building and yard, with many engines based at the sub-sheds at Aberystwyth, Portmadoc and Pwllheli. On 5 April 1960 No 5556 stands in the late morning sunshine. Also on shed the same day were Nos 2202, 5541, 3202, 7405, 6392, 5809, 2237, 2286, 78002 and 78006, with vintage 9015 in store. This is the western end, showing the original three-road edifice with slated gable-style pitched roof, erected by the Newtown & Machynlleth Railway and opened on 3 January 1863. Once again, appearances flatter to deceive. No 5556, a Machynlleth engine since October 1953, despite seemingly ready for the next duty, is dead, withdrawn the previous Boxing Day. *David Johnson*

Right Six years later, and seen from the 'Birmingham' end, No 78003 appears to be the subject of some discussion on 12 July 1966. Two roads of the old shed were through lines and the Cambrian Railway added an extension some time after absorbing the route in 1864, utilising these. The 'Standard' Class 2, standing on one of these roads, was new in November 1952 but not allocated until 24 January 1953, when it went to Oswestry. It was a widely travelled engine, being in and out of Wales on a number of occasions before settling at Shrewsbury (its allocation at this time) and ending its days on New Year's Eve 1966. Note the rebuilding that has fairly recently taken place on the shed building.

Above Pre-war views of locomotive sheds are, perhaps not surprisingly, much rarer than post-hostilities, but are the more fascinating for the distance in time and changes in circumstances and motive power. Around 1933 No 3726 stands at the shed entrance of the ex-LNWR facility at Nuneaton, next to 'Experiment' Class 4-6-0 No 25491 *Prince George*. Note the LMS '4' shedplate, denoting its home shed allocation. The second site for a depot at Nuneaton, this was initially opened as a four-road shed by the LNWR in 1878. It was doubled to eight roads ten years later and extended by 90 feet at the rear nine years after that. The roof was replaced around 1952 by an LMS-style louvre pitched roof with a brick screen, replacing the original glazed northlight pattern seen here. The depot closed on 6 June 1966. Built by Neilson Reid & Co in 1901 for the Midland as No 2697, the 0-6-0 was renumbered 3726 in 1907. It was allotted the number 58307 on nationalisation, but never actually bore that number and was finally withdrawn, from Monument Lane, on 2 December 1950. *MJS collection*

Left In a totally different part of the UK and from a quite different generation, No 3705 is coupled to a short rake of empty coal wagons in the shed yard at Newport (Pill) on 23 June 1963. The shed has obviously temporarily put the engine 'out to grass', as it was transferred to nearby Ebbw Junction the following week. Situated on the Monmouthshire branch at the north end of Alexandra Dock, Pill was a simple affair. A two-road brick-built structure, again with a northlight-pattern roof, there were but a handful of sidings in the yard. Built in 1898, it survived until 17 June 1965, being used for a while thereafter to stable diesel shunters. *David Richards*

Above Despite having the same allocation of 56 in 1950, the size and layout of Oxford's shed was the complete antithesis of Machynlleth (as seen on page 41). Its raison d'être, too, was in complete contrast, being in the midst of a busy north-south route that saw not only ex-GWR locos, but also visitors from four other Regions, and whose operations were a complete mix of passenger and freight workings. A spotter's paradise!

On 13 April 1965, as seen from the 6.52am Paddington-Birmingham (Snow Hill) DMU express service, locomotives are being prepared for the day's work ahead. 'Halls' and 2-6-2Ts predominate, reflecting the variety of duties, and are standing outside the three-road shed built by the West Midland Railway in 1862 as an addition to the original single-road facility opened by the Oxford, Worcester & Wolverhampton Railway in 1854; the latter building is that seen to the extreme left. Both survived until the end of steam at Oxford and the closure of the shed on 3 January 1966.

Below Seconds later, as the DMU moves past the shed, the yard is already alive with bustle and anticipation. Freight locos hold sway here, with Ray noting '9Fs', '8Fs', ex-LMS and 'Standard' Class 5s and ex-GWR pannier tanks. Apart from a few stabling sidings for Thames Turbos, all evidence of this sizeable layout has been obliterated, most recently by housing.

Above In many ways the humble 'Jinty' was the LMS equivalent of the GWR pannier tank, workaday but capable of plenty of hard work. On 18 August 1960 three examples stand ready to go at Rowsley shed. No 47460 has all the paraphernalia for a forthcoming turn, while 'sisters' Nos 47679 and 47459 stand tail-to-tail ahead of '9F' No 92138. Interestingly, No 47460, a Rowsley loco for the whole of its BR life, is here still wearing its 17D shedplate, despite the depot's code having been changed to 17C two years earlier! The loco was withdrawn on 18 May 1963. Both the other two pictured here were similarly parochial engines, No 47459 ending its days here on 26 January 1963 and 47679 on 10 August 1963. The four-road, twin-gable depot was opened in 1924, replacing the original site at the other end of Rowsley station. Closing in 1964 and subsequently demolished, the site is now happily being resurrected by the stalwarts of Peak Rail. *David Johnson*

Left On Westhouses shed on 31 March 1962, No 47638 also stands in the company of larger brethren, this time in the shape of one of Stanier's '8Fs'. Note the generic Midland shed design between here and Rowsley above. Opened in 1890, the shed was triple-pitched and had a ramped coal stage and 50-foot turntable. Closure came on 3 October 1966, with the site being used for some time as a diesel stabling point. No 47638 was more widely travelled than its Rowsley brethren above, moving around the Midlands area post-1948, before arriving at Westhouses on 6 January 1962. It was withdrawn less than two years later, on 13 July 1963. *MJS collection*

THE STEAM LOCOMOTIVE SHED

Above Another 'large' shed with a surprisingly small local allocation – a mere 57 in 1950 – was Salisbury. One of many depot sites in the city, this one was built in 1901 to replace a much altered one nearer to the station. A ten-road shed with five pitched slated roofs, it closed with the end of SR steam on 9 July 1967. On 9 August 1964 rebuilt and unrebuilt examples of Bulleid's 'light Pacifics' stand together on shed, both waiting their next turns. No 34014 *Budleigh Salterton* (left) perhaps looks more the part than No 34079 *141 Squadron* – here preparing for a run to Portsmouth Harbour – but both were equally capable of impressive performances. The former served at all points of the SR compass before being 'retired' from Salisbury on 12 April 1965, while *141 Squadron*, new at the beginning of August 1948, lived at only three depots – Ramsgate, Exmouth Junction and Eastleigh – before the end on 7 March 1966. In the background, modernity makes a bid in the guise of Nos 76067 and 76059.

Below By comparison, the scene just one year later, on 8 August 1965, is very different, although presenting the viewer with the same types and number of locos as above. Now there is a sense of a downturn in shed business and perhaps an over-supply of facilities. Left to right, we see Nos 34108 *Wincanton* (new on 20 May 1950), 76005 (8 January 1953), 76026 (10 December 1953) and, tender first, 34089 *602 Squadron* (31 January 1949). All survived to the end of steam on the SR. Ray records that, on this day, there were 30 locos on shed – including five diesels – but only seven steam engines actually in steam, together with one steam crane.

Here is an attractive but slightly unusual view of an 'A3' to close this section. On 17 April 1964 No 60051 *Blink Bonny* simmers quietly in Huddersfield (Hillhouse) yard, proudly sporting well-painted lining and the more modern of the two British Railways insignia on the tender. Obviously the recipient of 'TLC', she stands in the shed yard prepared for the following day's Gresley Society/Northern Railfans special to Derby and Crewe Works, which she worked from Huddersfield and back again. Built in 1924 and a well-travelled loco, belonging to Gateshead at this time (although wearing a 52B Heaton shedplate on the day of the tour!), the obvious care and attention sadly did little to preserve her for much longer, with withdrawal coming on 19 December 1964. The depot fared somewhat better. Opened originally by the LNWR in 1849 as a four-road dead-end shed, it was enlarged to six roads in 1882 and again to nine in 1905, with four of the tracks being opened to through running. A coaling plant was provided in 1937 to replace the original stage, and the end came on 2 January 1967. *MJS collection*

THE STEAM LOCOMOTIVE SHED

4.
REDHILL

Allocation in 1950: 30. Closed: 4 January 1965.

REDHILL.
The shed is in the fork of the Ashford and Brighton lines south of the station. The yard is visible from both lines.

Turn left outside the main entrance to the station (up side), and left again under the railway bridge along Station Road. This road bears to the right, and a broad path leads to the shed through the goods yard entrance on the right hand side, at the top of the hill. Walking time 5 minutes.

At the other end of the line from Reading (South) – already seen – Redhill was another of Ray Ruffell's favourite haunts. He spent many hours here and expended much film – the views in this section are but a sample.

Locomotive withdrawal and/or storage was ever a part of the railway's history, although probably never (with the possible exception of the ending of the Broad Gauge on the GWR) on the scale of the last 15/20 years of British Railways. On 23 October 1959 a group of engines stand 'dumped' at the rear of the shed, including, nearest the

camera, No 31247 ragged up and obviously not going anywhere fast! Interestingly, this 1903-vintage locomotive still wears a 73B shedplate, despite being transferred to 70A (Nine Elms) four months prior to this view. As both sheds were in London, it would be instructive to learn why the 'D1' found itself here at Redhill. Similarly, both No 31771 at the buffer stops and 31784 behind 31247 were due to be transferred to Nine Elms on 14 June 1959 – perhaps there was a temporary problem at the London shed preventing it accepting these immigrants.

Above Ray's caption to this is 'Freezing Weather'. We must take his word for it, but the snow on the ground and the weak winter sunshine of 15 January 1960 conspire to give a chill edge to the scene even now. No 31871 receives attention from its crew, including a presumably bitterly cold fireman handling the water bag, prior to leaving the shed and working a freight to Reading. 14 June 1959 must have been a momentous day on the SR, as many locomotives were moved between sheds on that date, including No 31871, which, despite coming to Redhill from Bricklayers Arms, still wears the previous 73B shedplate.

Below By 21 March 1960 those stored locos seen on the previous page have all been moved, to allow this 'open' shot of Nos 30836, 76054 and 31863, all 'in dock' and receiving remedial attention. The fitter sitting in the smokebox of the 'Standard', a broad smile on his lips, does not seem unduly stressed by his work! All the locomotives returned to give another 3-4 years' service. This view clearly shows the 1950 re-roofing that replaced the original slated gable style with a corrugated asbestos pitch over each road and similar material on this southern aspect.

Two days on from the previous view, No 76054 has obviously been 'put to rights' and is seen on the 'long pit' on 23 March 1960, being readied for the call. New in April 1955 from Doncaster Works and allocated to Redhill on 9 May, it stayed there for almost exactly five years. Some seven weeks after this shot, on 6 May 1960, it transferred westwards to Salisbury, from where it 'upped sticks' to Guildford on 22 June 1964. Withdrawal came while at that shed on 20 November 1964 – less than ten years old!

Above A vital part of many sheds was the turntable. The steam engine, by its very nature, was single-ended, and running 'chimney-first' was often preferable to the alternative. Tender engines especially did not find favour with crews asked to run in reverse, and no doubt the fireman seen here on 3 May 1960 is glad to be turning his charge, with the aid of vacuum from No 31880. Note the struts supporting the loco platform on this 1928 65-foot replacement of the earlier 45-foot version at a different site in the yard. The 1922 three-cylinder derivative of Maunsell's 'N' Class comprised only six examples – Nos 31822 and 31876-80. The last-numbered, seen here, like the rest of its fellows, was shedded at Hither Green for many years after nationalisation, eventually being moved on that fateful day in June 1959 to Tonbridge. From there it wandered to Stewarts Lane on 2 July 1962, only to be withdrawn four months later on 19 November.

Below As well as turning, food and drink was also important during a stay on shed, for both crew and loco. Also on 3 May 1960, No 31800 takes water before returning to the main line. Although looking very similar to the 'N1' above, the detail differences, especially in the shape of the cylinders and the presence of small splashers above the running plate, betray this as a 'U-boat'. One of the 20 1928 rebuilds of Maunsell's 'K' Class 'River' 2-6-4Ts, No 31800 spent its BR life moving to and from Guildford, its shed at the time of this view. It was withdrawn from there on 25 October 1965.

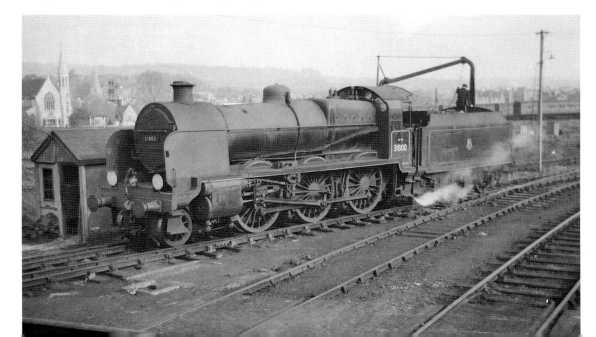

The vast majority of published views of Redhill shed are from the ground in the yard, or very occasionally from the surrounding hinterland. It is pleasing, therefore, to see this alternative aspect, captured by Ray travelling on the 7.23am Reading-Tonbridge train on Saturday 13 May 1961, showing just how close the shed was to the running line. In the yard are Nos 31616, 31876 and 31633, with 31872 dimly seen through the shed; Ray noted six other engines on shed, including No 31247 – seen stored in the view on page 47 – apparently still not having moved to Nine Elms! Note at this northern end the brick gable end and screen hiding the pitched roof, the unusual siting of the signal gantry almost within the confines of the shed yard, and the ramped coal stage (right), constructed in 1928.

THE STEAM LOCOMOTIVE SHED

Left Another view of the turntable, this time during the infamous hard winter of 1962/63. On 8 January 1963 leaden skies threaten more disruption as No 31638 takes its turn in providing vacuum for turning, surrounded by the remains of the snow that had begun falling on Boxing Day 1962! With the constant pounding of boots around the turntable, the snow appears to be turning to ice, promising to make the area even more treacherous! A well-travelled loco, No 31638 went to Guildford on 26 November 1959, from where withdrawal came on 27 January 1964.

Below left This second photograph of the shed on that bitterly cold day in January 1963 was taken from the top of an adjacent hill. The rear of the shed is seen once more, with No 31638 now off the turntable. No 30836 stands at the rear of the shed, obviously out of steam, in company with 'Schools' No 30930 *Radley*, which had been withdrawn just nine days earlier on 31 December. The extensive covering of snow throughout the town can be seen, as can the clear roof of the shed – no heat insulation here!

Below Looking towards the 'live' end of the shed, three 'Ns' stands ready for the road together with 'Standard' 2-6-4T No 80150. Trucks, tracks, houses and embankment are all blanketed in snow. The shed building changed little over the years from its construction by the South Eastern Railway in 1853, apart from the re-roofing by BR in 1950, with its relatively cramped position managing to cope with the demands placed upon it. As locos continued to use the site for some months after formal closure on 4 January 1965, it contrived to clock up 112 years of railway operation. No 80150, by contrast, emerging new from Brighton Works in December 1956 and being withdrawn on 31 October 1965, managed less than nine!

In this final look at Redhill and its turntable, the snows of two years earlier are now but a memory as fireman Earle takes advantage of the vacuum to turn No 31639 on 4 September 1965, having worked in with the 'Blisworth Parcels'. Closed now to steam, the calls of Reading-Redhill trains needed answering, hence the continued use of the available facilities. Viewed from the end of the 'coal plant road', No 31639, the last of the batch of 'U' Class locos built with smaller splashers and other detail differences, has lost its shedplate but is yet another Guildford incumbent. Truly looking the part here, it survived for another nine months, finally condemned to death on 27 June 1966.

5.
...AND LARGE

Compared to contemporaries in the capital, such as Nine Elms, Stewarts Lane, Old Oak Common, Willesden, Stratford or King's Cross, Bricklayers Arms was a 'forgotten' shed, but those who did make the trip were greeted by a wealth of variety. There were large and small, older and younger, but undoubtedly one of the appeals was the presence of Bulleid's 'Pacifics' allocated and/or serviced there. Graphically making the point in 1958 is No 34003 *Plymouth*, fresh from Brighton Works in June 1945 and here only months from its conversion from Bulleid's original streamline state in September 1957. A similarly rebuilt sister loco stands quietly simmering behind. The fireman looks proud to be on the footplate of this shining example. The layout of the depot was strung out both in time and place, with many alterations, additions and subtractions over the years. In this view, the two Bulleids stand outside the 1865 four-road addition to the 1847 building, also with four roads. The latter's northlight-pattern roof was a 1937 provision, whereas the corrugated asbestos louvre pitched style, on the left, was a relatively late provision in 1952. *Norman Gurley, MJS collection*

Above Bristol (Bath Road) was a large shed in all respects. With an allocation in three figures, and occupying a wide swathe of land immediately adjacent to the southern end of Temple Meads station, it was a wondrous place for spotters to either visit or merely gaze upon from the platform end! Happily, developments at the station in the mid-1930s brought such spotters closer to the shed buildings, enabling views such as this of No 3433 backing on to the shed around 1936. The building seen on the right was opened in 1934, a 10-road replacement for the two-road edifice that occupied this part of the yard (note also the newness of the shed to the left of the water tower), and the station saw development completed in 1935. An un-named member of the GWR 'Bulldog' Class of 4-4-0s, No 3433, built in 1906,

was initially numbered 3723 until 1912. It was withdrawn in April 1939. *MJS collection*

Below The steam shed at Bath Road was closed on 12 September 1960, demolished and the site redeveloped with a purpose-built diesel depot. Not surprisingly, the architectural style for the 'boxes on wheels' was totally at odds with that for their predecessors, one example, seen here, providing a concrete and glass backdrop. All manner of diesel types are on show in this shot from an Open Day in 1965, but variety is provided by steam, notably the specially cleaned No 44856 visiting from the LMR. Recently transferred to the ex-GWR depot at Oxley, on the outskirts of Wolverhampton, it survived until 25 February 1967. *MJS collection*

Above Despite there being three operational sheds in Carlisle during the 1950s, Kingmoor still managed to combine sheer size and allocation numbers to rank as a massive shed. Sprawling at the eastern side of the main line, north of the city, just some of the appeal to the average enthusiast can be seen in this view of the north yard on 1 April 1967, as the overcoated enthusiast on the right leads our eye to the yard. Less than a year before closure on 1 January 1968, and only 16 months from the very end of steam on BR, the number of locos and the activity depicted here could have been from almost any previous period. Kingmoor was an eight-road facility throughout its life, originally opening in 1876 and enjoying rebuilding in 1916. Note the massive slab of the mechanical coaling plant (left),

erected by the LMS in 1937. Sadly, Ray did not record the engine numbers, but certainly present are a number of 'Britannias', including what appears to be the un-named No 70047, 'Black Fives', and LMS 2-6-0 'Pigs'.

Below In some ways the south end always seemed the quieter yard, but was, nevertheless, equally as interesting in terms of the locomotives present. On the same day as above, Stanier's influence stands cheek-by-jowl with Type 1, 2 and 4 diesels, one of which Ray has noted as being 'in steam'! The twin pitched roofs to the right of the main shed shelters the four-road repair shop. Enthusiasts wander with cameras around their necks, but none appear to be using them in anger!

At the time of writing, the Great Western Society at Didcot is involved in 'retro-building' No 4942 *Maindy Hall* into a 'Saint', reversing the conversion initially set in motion by *Saint Martin*. Here is that original, seen by the substantial coaling stage on Old Oak Common shed in July 1926, before being renumbered to formally become the first 'Hall', but still retaining the name. Originally built in 1907, it had been 'tweaked' from its original 'Saint' status in 1924 by merely replacing the 6ft 8½in wheels with 6-foot ones and fitting a side-window cab. Entering the world in its new guise in December 1924, it was renumbered exactly four years later, at the time that the new 'Halls' began to appear. *MJS collection*

THE STEAM LOCOMOTIVE SHED

Above On the SR, Eastleigh was head and shoulders above its contemporaries in importance. Not only was there the Works rubbing shoulders with the running shed, but also the latter enjoyed an allocation in 1950 of 145, nearly 20 per cent more than Exmouth Junction, its nearest rival. No 30120 is one of those fortunate locos that escaped the cutter's torch, but when seen by Ray on 24 July 1961 it was merely just another engine operating from Exmouth Junction. Emerging from Nine Elms Works in August 1899 as the eighth-built 'T9', it was fitted with superheaters in May 1927 and gave steady but largely unremarkable service in the south-west of the SR until finally going cold in July 1963.

Below Seen at the other end of the shed on 30 April 1965, No 31790 stands prepared and ready for the next run, with the fireman checking the tender locker. He wouldn't have to check it many more times on this Guildford loco, however, as the fire was dropped for withdrawal on 6 June. Built to replace two small sheds sited closer to Eastleigh station, the L&SWR 15-road shed was newly built in open fields, opening on 1 January 1903. To the east of the line to Southampton, the roof was originally of slate and glazing construction, but this was replaced by BR around 1950 with the ubiquitous corrugated asbestos. It closed with the end of steam on the SR on 9 July 1967, and the site was thereafter redeveloped for dieselisation.

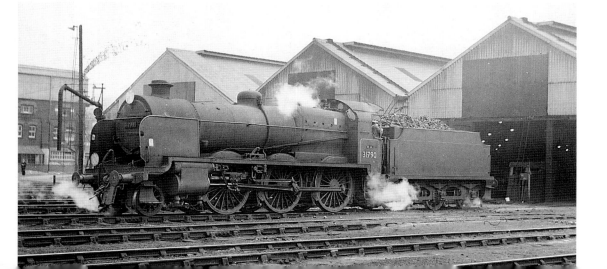

Above Two more shots of Eastleigh, the first taken at the south end on 2 March 1966. As can be seen, each of the pitched roof spans covered three tracks; however, despite the number of locos allocated here, the undercover facilities were limited. Perhaps because they were expected to be rapidly turned round, most of a visiting, or even local, loco's time was spent at the mercy of the elements. The shed yard here gives space to stored locos, including Nos 33006, 33020, 80142, 34048 *Crediton*, 76019, 73016, 34079 *141 Squadron* and 34041 *Wilton*. Most are already withdrawn or, like No 80142 nearest the camera, soon will be. This engine, new in June 1956, met its end on 2 May 1966, not yet ten years old!

Below Again at the other end, this time the last day is obviously approaching. Photographed by Ray from a passing train on 7 July 1967, two days away from the very end, a mere four steamers are in view – none actually in steam – in company with an equal number of diesels. No 34040 *Crewkerne*, on the left at the end of the short row of stored locos, will work no more for BR. A sign of the times!

THE STEAM LOCOMOTIVE SHED

While most enthusiasts visited sheds for loco numbers and/or photography, there was, in truth, much else to see and enjoy. It is perhaps only in retrospect that much of the latter appeal has become apparent, but some of the infrastructure that most of us took for granted and never gave a second glance is captured here by Ray, aboard the 'Merchant Navy'-hauled 4.55pm Exeter (Central)-Waterloo express on Sunday 14 October 1962 passing Exmouth Junction. The shed building stands smack in the centre of this view, partly veiled by the steam emitted by some of the many locos on shed, but the yard lights, coaler, yardmen's huts and goods wagons all greatly contribute to the whole. Situated north of the main line, 1¼ miles east of Exeter (Queen Street/Central) station, the original 11-road through shed was constructed by the L&SWR in 1887, opening on 3 November. Strangely for such an important location, the shed was made of corrugated iron and this led to its eventual demise in 1927. The 12-road concrete slab that replaced it, slightly to the east, had the luxury of a mechanical coaler, seen just to the left of Ray's train. Closure came in March 1967.

THE STEAM LOCOMOTIVE SHED

Above left As well as the appeal already highlighted, sheds also often gave an opportunity to come close to examples of elderly engines that no longer stretched their legs on the main line. One such, No 69377, an example of T. W. Worsdell's NER Class 'B' 0-6-2Ts (LNER 'N8'), is seen in the shed yard at Heaton on 27 August 1954. Moving but little in BR days – allocated only to Hull (Dairycoates) and Heaton – No 69377 was one of a class of 62 locos introduced by Worsdell from 1886. Originally two-cylinder compounds, all were converted to 'simples' at a later date, and some were fitted with superheaters and/or piston valves. The class was extinct by 1956 (No 69390 going on 20 October of that year), with '77 surviving to 23 July 1955. *Brian Morrison*

Left On the same day, another tank, although of a much more recent vintage, shunts around the yard at Heaton, while in the background No 60146 *Peregrine* receives a fresh load of coal from the manhandled tipper wagon. One of several hundred 'Austerity' 0-6-0STs ordered by the Ministry of Supply from Hunslet and others to support the war effort, No 68014 emerging blinking into the dark world of September 1944 as No 75134 (Hunslet Works No 3184). Purchased by the LNER in July 1946 and numbered 8014, it became 68014 after nationalisation and spent all its BR life in the North East, working from Heaton, Blaydon and Darlington. The end came at the latter on 17 October 1964. *Brian Morrison*

Above Heaton stood next to the main line, north of Newcastle station, as can be seen here on 27 August 1954 as No 60810 guides a fitted freight bound for York past No 43016, waiting to leave the confines of the shed yard. Sited east of Heaton station, in the fork between lines to Edinburgh and North Shields, the NER built a three-road brick facility in 1875. Enlarged to eight roads in 1889, but still dead-end, the five tracks closest to the main line 'broke out' through the shed wall in 1931 and the most northernmost of these can be seen on the right. Apart from housing electric locos Nos 26500 and 26501 for a time, the shed closed on 17 June 1963. Demolition came in the 1970s, the site being redeveloped for diesels, mostly multiple units. *Brian Morrison*

...AND LARGE

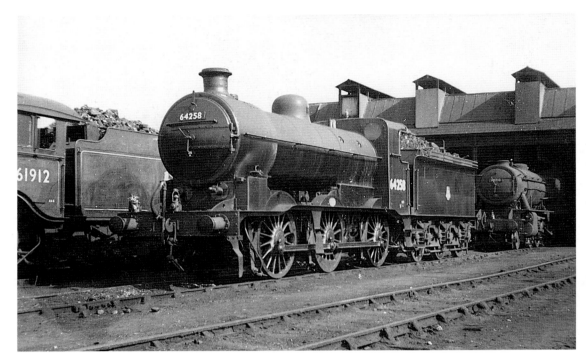

Above While many sheds were in the midst of towns and/or built-up areas, there were also a large number 'in the middle of nowhere'. March was one such, in the wilds of the Fens and on a spur from a huge marshalling yard on the outskirts of the relatively small community. Built there by the GER as a six-road shed in 1884, to replace the much sparser accommodation at the west end of March station, the LNER added a further four tracks under cover alongside the north wall of the existing building in 1925. 1933 saw an additional five-road structure erected next to the marshalling yard, officially as a wash-out facility, but general loco servicing was also undertaken there, and it is this building that is photographed here, evidenced by the northlight-pattern roof. On 13 May 1956 No 64258 stands temporarily out of steam but proudly in near-pristine condition at the entrance to the shed building, in company with Nos 61912 and 90210. One of the Gresley-designed 'J6' Class, No 64258 was a home-loving loco, residing at Doncaster for the whole of its BR career until its demise on 23 May 1959. *David Johnson*

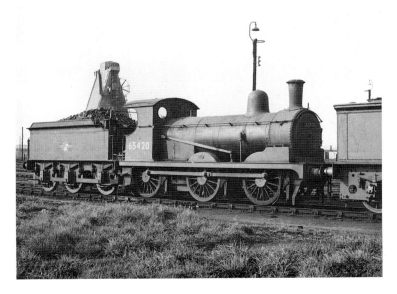

Left Even after the influx of 'B1s', then 'Britannias', elderly ex-LNER locos continued to ply their trade from March. On 4 May 1958 No 65420 is also out of steam, but, with the healthy coal supply in the tender, not for long. A long-term frequenter of East Anglian routes, and allocated to March at the time of this shot, it eventually moved south to Stratford on 23 June 1962, only to suffer the indignity of an early rejection, being withdrawn less than two months later on 11 August. Not the 'cenotaph' (mechanical coaler) behind, installed in 1925, and the ex-LNWR tender to the right on No 65420. Presumably an 0-8-0 had worked in from Northampton or Rugby, via Peterborough East. *J. K. Morton/MJS collection*

THE STEAM LOCOMOTIVE SHED

Above In another shot from Ray's camera on board a passing train – this time a 'Deltic'-hauled London-bound express - we see No 60854 at the head of a line of stored locos in the yard at New England, Peterborough, on 26 July 1963. A servant of the ECML for most of its working days, No 60854 did spend six months away, at Leicester (Central) shed, between September 1957 and March 1958, but most of its duties were from New England or Grantham depots. Returning home to Peterborough in April 1963, it had been withdrawn a fortnight when Ray photographed it. The original six-road main shed building can be seen to the left, under the signal gantry, while the later three-road addition is beyond the line of locos. The shed closed to steam in January 1965, the site being given over to diesels, but only until 30 September 1968, after which the depot was demolished and the site redeveloped for non-railway use.

Below Echoing the predilection of Eastleigh, Peterborough and others for stabling locos outside, Newport (Ebbw Junction) seems to have absolutely no spare space on 19 June 1949. The shed was home to many tender locos, but here the scene is completely filled by tanks, with that on the extreme right being one of those that escaped cutting but was just one of the boys back then. No 4247 has its number captured by the oldish and sedate spotter on the left – note the 'polite' dress of his accomplices! With an allocation of 143 in 1950, the depot needed all this space. Opened late in railway terms, in July 1915, it included a large repair shop, seen in the centre with its myriad windows. Closure came, in line with the elimination of steam from the WR, in October 1965. *John Edgington*

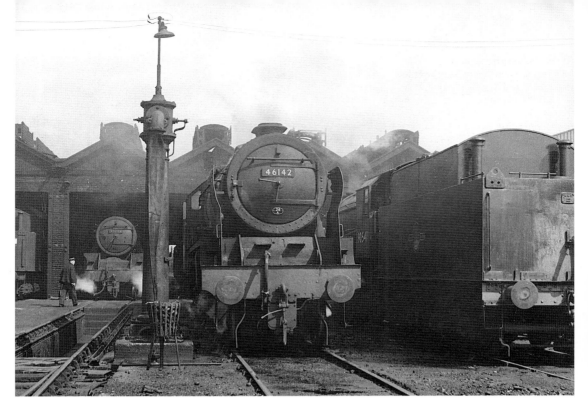

Above One of my delights, as a spotter during shed visits, was to see 'namers' and freight locos side by side. Newton Heath, a large shed just to the south of Manchester (Victoria) station, with its massive width of 24 tracks (23 of them straight through!), was one of many sheds where this variety could be enjoyed. Opened by the L&YR in 1876, it boasted two coaling stages and two 42-foot turntables. A large part of the southern half of the shed was demolished in 1959, to leave room for a purpose-built DMU servicing facility, with the northern half going in 1969, after the depot had closed to steam on 1 February 1968. On 14 April 1962 No 46142 *The York & Lancaster Regiment* waits purposefully by the water column, with No 90541 also enjoying the spring sunshine, while No 45739 *Ulster* looks ready to leave the shed confines. All had many months of active service remaining. *J. K. Morton/MJS collection*

Left On the same day, No 42981, looking smart in fine lined condition, simmers in readiness to return to its home shed of Birkenhead. Though many crews preferred the Hughes 'Crab' 2-6-0s to these Stanier versions, and it is true many of the latter suffered an unhealthy number of problems, members of the class still lasted until the end of steam and worked alongside their predecessors to the close. In 1961/62 many were transferred to Nuneaton depot, as it was felt that they would receive better maintenance there, but the local crews were not enamoured and after 'representations to management' they all eventually moved on. No 42981 went there on 16 June 1962, only to retreat back north to Crewe (South) one year later. Withdrawal was in May 1966, from Heaton Mersey. *J. K. Morton/MJS collection*

THE STEAM LOCOMOTIVE SHED

Right We have mentioned Nine Elms before, so we now look at the shed that Ray called 'Steam Capital of the World'! Comparison of locos was another facet of shed visits, not least in nose-to-nose encounters. On 6 February 1964 No 30111, acting as shed pilot, undertakes a little yard shunting with a 'Standard' 2-6-2T. A Bournemouth engine for the whole of its BR existence – and wearing the appropriate 71B shedplate here – it had been withdrawn ten days prior to this shot; presumably Nine Elms had appropriated it to cover a shortage of its own motive power.

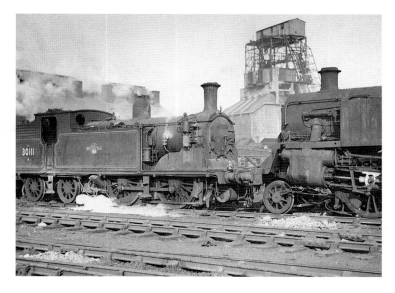

Below Here are two more fronts on the same day, but inviting comparison of a different sort. On the left, No 34085 *501 Squadron*, one of the rebuilt versions of Bulleid's inventions, stands outside the 10-road 'New Shed' (opened in 1910 on the eastern edge of the original 1885 15-road building) in company with an original, unrebuilt sister, No 34102 *Lapford* – arguments still rage as to which type was preferable. New, respectively, in January 1949 and March 1950, they ended their days at Bournemouth on 25 October 1965 and Eastleigh on 9 July 1967 – interesting that the unrebuilt version survived the longest! Note the AWS battery box neatly tucked away above the buffer beam.

Above Widening the angle of view, the shed yard at Nine Elms is seen here on 20 August 1963 from the vantage point of the turntable at the south-western corner of the yard, with yet more 'light Pacifics' on view. No 34044 *Woolacombe* quenches its thirst, while behind No 34058 *Sir Frederick Pile* waits its turn, having just come off the table ready to be positioned under the coaling plant. *Woolacombe* was yet another Bournemouth loco, working through to close to the end, being withdrawn on 12 June 1967.

Below Almost without exception, published views of Nine Elms have been on the ground, within the boundaries of the shed, and to my knowledge none have previously shown this angle. Again captured by Ray from a passing train – a 'down fast Pompey' – on 7 July 1967, this is view of the back of the shed, with a 2-6-2T, a Bulleid 'Pacific' with steam to spare, and a diesel shunter (later Class 08) in view, but the sheer variety of infrastructure detail is the most interesting facet. The depot closed two days later, and the site was later redeveloped as a replacement for the Covent Garden fruit and vegetable market.

THE STEAM LOCOMOTIVE SHED

Above Usually, the 'A' shed of any code was the most important, with the largest allocation. Not so the '84s' in 1950. Wolverhampton (Stafford Road) was the parent shed, but no fewer than five others within the group outshone it in numbers. Perhaps strangely, it was Shrewsbury, well down the list as 84G in 1950, that was way out in front with 122 resident locos – probably a legacy of being 'two sheds in one', belonging to the former GWR and LNWR. Once more Ray has taken the opportunity of travelling by train to record what he saw from the carriage windows. Seen from the 'Cambrian Coast Express' of 9 July 1966, No 75016 heads the yard line-up, with Nos 45311 and 78018 immediately behind, all obviously raring to go!

Below A few seconds later the 1877 ex-LNWR part of the shed is seen, with No 92218 on the left and No 44926 on the right; the 1883 ex-GWR facility stood to the left of the LNWR in this view. Shrewsbury was one of a small handful of locations where sizeable sheds of competing companies were sited adjacent to one another, and certainly under their original parentage – and to a large degree after nationalisation – the locos of each company kept to their 'own side', even though the shed access road, by Coleham signal box, was common to both! These two views show something of the nature of the set-up and the resulting acreage of railway land. Having come under WR control at nationalisation, the LMR finally had the last laugh, taking over the reins in 1963, with the code becoming 6D, under Chester's umbrella. The whole edifice closed to steam on 6 November 1967, being used for diesel servicing until 1972.

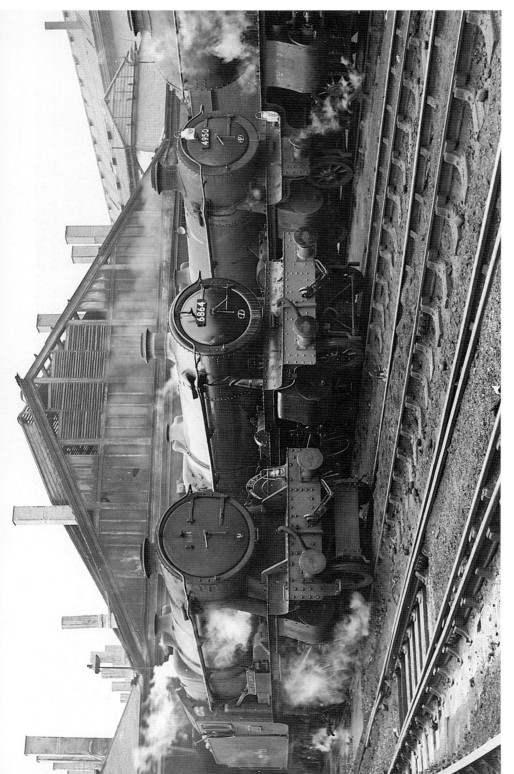

Of all sheds, one of the greatest favourites of all with enthusiasts was Swindon. Reasons are many and various, but certainly to this Midland spotter it was Mecca, with those glamorous and gleaming green, copper and brass locos with individual cabside number plates and no regional prefixes to their original pre-nationalisation numbers. An almost typical view is that captured on 1 December 1963, with ex-Works No 6864 *Dymock Grange* sandwiched between two fellow, but grimy, neighbours outside the 1871-vintage nine-road shed; the 1908 'extension' shows its younger age on the right. No 1014 *County of Glamorgan* has had the indignity of losing its front number plate, a fate spared No 4950 *Patshull Hall*; the front end of No 1013 *County of Dorset* just squeezes into the picture on the right. The two 'Counties' and the 'Hall' lasted until the following summer, but No 6864 was more successful, continuing until 9 October 1965. *Hugh Ballantyne*

THE STEAM LOCOMOTIVE SHED

Above With its smokebox lock absent, No 44833 is not about to move from the smoke and grime of Willesden yard on 17 January 1965, whereas No 76041 looks well ready for the fight; both locomotives survived until 1967. The smokebox of No 78019 pokes into view on the left. *Hugh Ballantyne*

Below In a single image this view of Willesden encapsulates so much of the appeal of the steam shed: locos left and right, in steam; lots of numbers; a wide variety; and the sheer taste of the atmosphere, once savoured, never forgotten. On 10 June 1964 a selection from the yard includes Nos 45056, 45328, 42431, 48479, 78033 (tender first), 73033, and 47501 next to the canal. The building outside which they stand is the original 1873 LNWR 12-road dead-end shed. In 1898 a 12-road extension was added to this (western) end, but due to its rapidly deteriorating state it was demolished in 1939, leaving just the earlier attractive triple-hipped slate roof. To the left can be seen the outline of the brick-built square roundhouse, provided in 1929. The whole site was closed on 27 August 1965 and demolished, later to become a Freightliner terminal. *Hugh Ballantyne*

Another great favourite with enthusiasts from all over the country was York, with the extra delight here of two distinct sizeable sheds of equal appeal. Taken by Ray from the passing northbound 'Heart of Midlothian' express, this view of the North shed on 26 June 1965 has ER and LMR steam passenger and freight types adding to the pollution and no doubt making it difficult for the local populace to maintain clean washing-lines! Both the sites at York, north and south of the station, saw many changes, developments and amendments over the years, and their history makes fascinating reading for long winter evenings!

THE STEAM LOCOMOTIVE SHED

6.
CARNFORTH

Allocation in 1950: 42. Closed: 5 August 1968.

CARNFORTH 11A.

The shed is on the west side of the Barrow line north west of the station. The yard is visible from the line.

Turn left outside the station into Warton Road, and after about 150 yards left again over a foot-bridge. This leads to the shed. Walking time 5 minutes.

Ray made just two trips to Carnforth, one year apart, in December 1966 and 1967. A narrow view as this may be, it does give an interesting perspective on progress with and within the shed. Viewed from the south on 3 December 1966, No 92128, sans front number plate, receives replenishment from the 1944 mechanical coaling plant. The '9F' is no surprise, but the Derby Lightweight DMU is a more unusual sight here. The tracks in the foreground led to three headshunts and access to an exit road, in the bottom left-hand corner of this view.

An outstanding feature of Ray's 1966 visit was the presence of so many locomotives literally fired up and displaying their eagerness! One such was Carlisle (Kingmoor)-based No 45455, complete with mini-snowplough and stencilled shed code, seemingly demanding both attention and a way to the open road. 'Standard' Class 5 No 73157 and another 'Black Five' wait their turn. Part of a batch of 'Black Fives' built at Crewe in 1938, No 45455 was one of a handful of the class that stubbornly remained at just one depot throughout BR's steam existence, being withdrawn from Kingmoor on 9 September 1967.

THE STEAM LOCOMOTIVE SHED

Right In the first of two further views of No 92128, the '9F', having been coaled and watered, runs round the shed to the north end, expelling excess steam along the way. New in April 1957 to Toton, it progressively served Leicester (Midland), Saltley, Banbury, Saltley (again) and, finally, Carnforth. Arrival here was on 12 November 1966, less than a month prior to this portrait. Note how the stencilled '2D' code – denoting Banbury, where it had been between 18 July 1964 and 10 September 1966 – has not been obliterated or covered with an appropriate 10A shedplate.

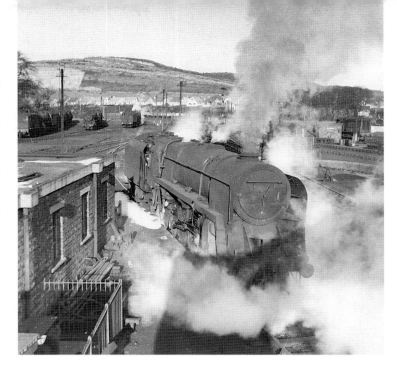

Below A few moments later the loco is back on the south side and in position at the shed entrance to wait for the next call. The lack of a smokebox numberplate and that stencilled, out-of-date coding might lead one to expect that No 92128 was near the end, but this was not so, as withdrawal did not come for a further 12 months, on 2 December 1967 – another criminal waste of a valuable asset, at a little over ten years old and barely 'run in'! 'Mickey Mouse' No 46433 – another Carnforth loco - and an unidentified 08 diesel shunter stand alongside.

And so to the second visit. On 30 December 1967, not only is the weather a contrast – rain instead of the previous year's sunshine – but the whole atmosphere on the shed is totally changed. Looking south from the footbridge, gone are the angry steam engines, replaced by rows of cold, redundant stock and the spread of dieselisation. An 08 shunts empty wagons, while a solitary 'Black Five' clings to life on the extreme left, close to the main line.

THE STEAM LOCOMOTIVE SHED

Right Evidence of the quietness of the shed on this day is epitomised by No 92167, cold and damp and out of steam, alongside the new regime in the guise of D216 *Campania*. Note the 'W' on the diesel's cabside, denoting its allocation to the Western Division of the LMR. Happily, at this time, the '9F' is still in capital stock. It was delivered new in May 1958 to Saltley depot in Birmingham, one of just three – the others being Nos 92165/6 – fitted with a mechanical stoker and double chimney. From there it travelled to the NER and Tyne Dock depot on 12 May 1962, but for just five months, coming home to Saltley on 20 October of that year. A move to Bidston followed in December 1962, thence to Birkenhead in February

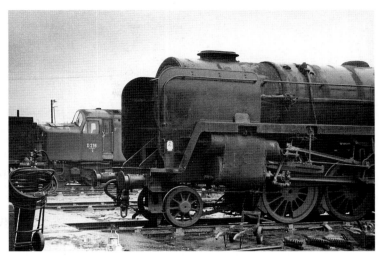

1963 and, finally, to Carnforth on 11 November 1967, where it ended its life on 13 July 1968, just three weeks before the end of steam on BR. D216 was new from Vulcan Foundry in June 1959, its first allocation being Crewe North on 18 July. After moving through various allocations, its end came in the 1980s – withdrawn from Carlisle Kingmoor in May 1981 and cut at Swindon Works in November 1983.

Below Elsewhere in the yard, No 44758 waits under the ash disposal plant, with the depressing weather equally depressing the smoke and steam – no more angry scenes here! No 44758 appeared new from Crewe in 1947, complete with Timken roller bearings throughout, but still with a single chimney. Crewe (North) was its first home, where it stayed until June 1959. Movements were more frequent thereafter, until the final one, to Carnforth, on 23 April 1966. It survived, however, to share in the very end of BR steam in August 1968.

Above A link with a bygone past. When Fowler took over the reins at Derby, one of his first products was an 0-6-0 in the mould of his predecessors. The first examples saw life in 1911, with the production line beginning in earnest in 1917 and ending with No 4026 in 1922. Two years later he let rip with a type that would eventually spawn 580 examples (and, after 1928, classified '4F' as opposed to just '4'). No 44027, here a sight for sore eyes among its more modern brethren, was the first, appearing in 1924; while not the last of its type to survive, it certainly soldiered on gamely until late into class withdrawals, the end coming on 28 November 1964 at Barrow-in-Furness. The loco looks remarkably intact here, three years later, as she escaped the cutter's attentions and became beloved of the Midland Railway Centre at Butterley, as part of the National Collection.

Below With its smoke swirling in the damp wind, No 45095 earns its crust by shunting No 44711, ready to be positioned for a boiler washout. '95 was another well-travelled 'Black Five', from Glasgow southwards, eventually lighting at Carnforth on 9 May 1964 and going on to survive to the end of steam on BR in 1968. The younger No 44711 – new in October 1948 – also lived until late in the day, but did not quite make the final party, being withdrawn on 18 May 1968.

This second view from the footbridge is looking north and focuses on the sidings and the scrap line. With diesels rapidly taking over the former steam duties, the shed building increasingly became a preserve of the former, their steam counterparts being relegated to the mercies of the open air – after all, the end was in sight. The 70-foot turntable about to be invaded by the Type 4s was installed by the LMS when the new shed was placed here, on the site of the previous Furness Railway facility, in 1944.

Above The ends are truly in sight in this close-up view of the scrap lines at the northern extremities of the shed. Almost exclusively 'Standards' in this view, the rejection of so much potential and the under-utilisation of investment was little short of criminal, in the unholy rush to rid the network of steam.

Below Its days are numbered but No 92249 hangs on, without front number or shedplate, and with obviously little attention to the superstructure. New in December 1958, to Newport (Ebbw Junction), homes were subsequently made at Plymouth (Laira), Ebbw Junction again, Newton Heath from 12 October 1963, Carlisle (Kingmoor), and finally Speke Junction. Despite the lack of relevant information on the smokebox, this was the allocation at the date of this shot. The loco was withdrawn from Speke on 18 May 1968, following the closure of that shed earlier in the month. 'Britannia' No 70021 *Morning Star*, beyond, certainly has an ironic misnomer at this date, having just been withdrawn!

THE STEAM LOCOMOTIVE SHED

7.
INSIDE

While illustrations of shed buildings, yards and their occupants are common, views on the inside are not so frequently seen. These two views of Blackpool (Central) demonstrate both the latent appeal and the photographic challenge. The first shows *Seahorse* in store. Although ex-Works, 'Jubilee' No 45705 is out of steam and out of work on 19 January 1963. Note how the prevailing light conditions of the steel and glass transverse pitched roof, installed as late as 1957, challenge the film to faithfully record areas of highlight and shadow. Originally a four-road shed in 1863, the L&YR replaced it with an eight-road building in 1885; formal closure came on 2 November 1964, but facilities remained for a period afterwards, to give shelter and attention to visiting locomotives. As for *Seahorse*, a long-time resident of Farnley Junction, it came to Blackpool on 16 June 1956. Eighteen months after this view, transfer was made to Newton Heath on 20 June 1964, from where the end came on 6 November 1965. *Peter Fitton*

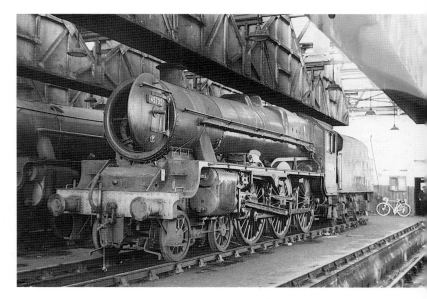

Visiting locomotives not infrequently arrived on shed in less than 100 per cent health, needing remedial attention from their temporary home. Whether this was the cause of Wakefield's 'B1' No 61123 being on shed is unknown, but by the look of things on 29 August 1964 it is ready for the return across the Pennines, which is more than can be said for the 'Black Five' with stripped motion and cylinders behind. D228 *Samaria* stands on the next line. *Peter Fitton*

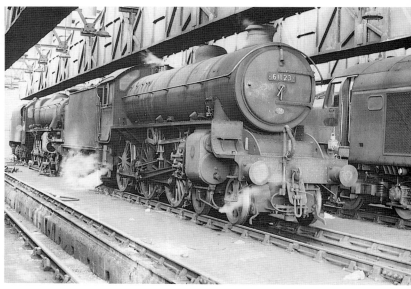

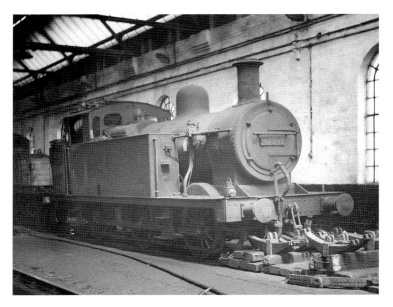

Left The proximity of the windows and the inherent Stygian gloom within again demonstrate the technical problems of inside photography. With a hand-held exposure of 1/25th second, Ray has done well to record No 47348, obviously out of work at Bletchley, trapped as it is between the wagon and the collection of springs, despite the pile of coal atop the cab! Introduced in October 1935, one of 422 Fowler Class 3 0-6-0Ts, No 47348 came to BR at Devons Road (Bow). Arrival at Bletchley was on 7 November 1959, after a brief sojourn at Camden, but officially the allocation was transferred to Wolverton Works from 30 April 1960. On 25 July 1962, however, the 'Jinty' is still at Bletchley, though in store. Formal withdrawal came two months after this, on 8 September.

Below Elsewhere in the shed that day, other engines are 'in service' but not in steam. Again captured at 1/25th second, No 48550, closest to the camera on the right, lines up with Nos 42105, 75028 and 48205, with grease and the giveaway raised frame of No 75038 on the left. Only the two '8Fs' were visitors, but all had been dispersed 'to the four winds' by withdrawal. Originally a three-road shed, later enlarged to six tracks, yet another BR replacement roof – this time glass louvres with a brick end screen – was provided in 1954, but only provided shelter for some 11 years, the depot closing on 15 July 1965.

THE STEAM LOCOMOTIVE SHED

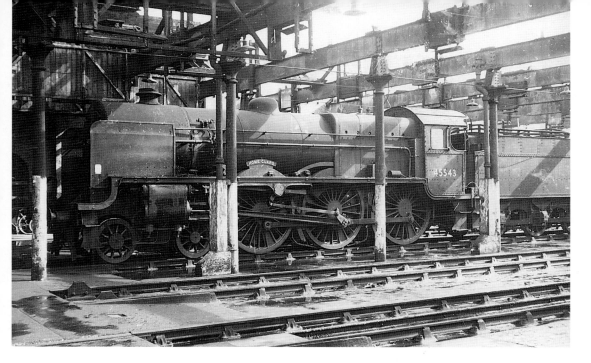

Above Yes, this is inside! In happier times, No 45543 *Home Guard* would have been under the protection of the overall roof at Preston, but after the infamous roof fire of 28 June 1960 not only was the shed closed (from 12 September 1961) but also locos stored there in the short term were 'in the open'. The sun shines brightly on the ruins on 16 September 1962. Several 'Patriots' saw 'shelter' here in this period, together with a mixed handful of other locos. *Home Guard* spent most of its BR existence split between Crewe (North) and Carlisle (Upperby), before flitting between Preston, Longsight, Edge Hill, Lancaster and Carnforth. Nominally at the latter from 2 June 1962, the shed did not receive value from its asset, as this view shows it in store, prior to official withdrawal on 1 December. One of several depots in Preston, the ex-LNWR facility was once a 15-track affair, but had been reduced to nine roads by the time of the fire. *Peter Fitton*

Below By way of contrast, this is inside looking out. The sun is most definitely not shining here at Bolton, as 'Standard' Class 5s and Stanier '8Fs' peer out at or stand in the inclement conditions on 23 March 1968. The weather and the pools of water on the walkways between the pits all add to the feel of times having been better, less than five months from the end of steam. Originally a four-road structure, enlargement to double that size came in 1888. A louvre roof with a brick screen, similar to that at Bletchley, was installed by the LMS in 1946, but the gloom here prevents appreciation! Closure came on 1 July 1968, one month from the very end of steam on BR.

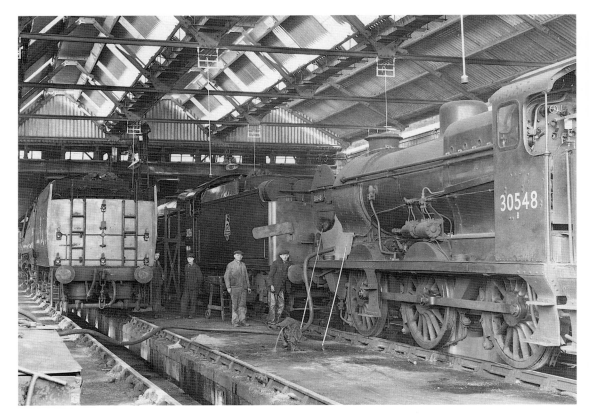

Above The work involved in the rebuilding of Bournemouth shed has already been seen on page 37, where on 4 March 1953 we glimpsed the rear of No 30548. Here is a further view of the loco on that day. New in September 1939 – allocated to Nine Elms and just in time for the war! – it is here receiving the fitters' attention despite the work obviously continuing on the roof above. Note the presence of the workman on the crossbeam above the Bulleid's tender, and the ex-SR 'B' cabside classification – surely overdue for replacement by BR's '4F' by this time? Ahead of the 'Q' Class locomotive, 'Lord Nelson' No 30861 *Lord Anson* looks to be recently ex-Works, with the tender sheets and boiler cladding shining and the attractive lining clean and unimpaired. The grime of the overalls stands out by comparison, and note the water hydrant between the tracks gaily cascading on to the walkway! *MJS collection*

Above right The name Bournville is inexorably linked with Cadbury's, both for the factory and the chocolate that it produced. The factory created much work for the railway and the MR provided an engine shed to cope on the west side of the line, south of Bournville station. Opened in 1895, its roundhouse tracks were entombed within a brick square and triple-pitch slate roof. In the months immediately prior to nationalisation, a wonderful line-up of ex-MR and LMS types obligingly faces the turntable, basking in the shafts of warm summer sun. Left to right on 7 August 1947 are Nos 78, 1064, 22863, 439 and 3583, all quietly resting on their home turf. Pride of place in the view goes to No 22863. Built in March 1874 by Dübs & Co as No 1063, it became 2863 in the 1907 renumbering. It was fitted with a D boiler and 18-inch cylinders in April 1908, then a G6 boiler in March 1923 – the type seen fitted here. Renumbered to 22863 in April 1934, it was to become 58113 in BR service, but was withdrawn in January 1949 before it could do so. *Neville Stead collection/MJS collection*

Right Anyone who has attempted in-shed photography will sympathise with Ray in his challenge with this shot. Duly recorded as 1/25th second at f3.5 and 30 feet distance, the depth of field is necessarily limited and No 48775 does not aid the situation by virtue of the copious steam effects! This is the inside of Buxton shed on 24 March 1968, one week from closure, with a Type 2 diesel and one of the depot's snowploughs to the right. No 48775 had a chequered career. Built at Crewe in 1937 as LMS 8025, it was one of 51 '8Fs' requisitioned by the WD in 1941 and renumbered 583. It returned to capital stock – along with Nos 48773 and 48774 (ex-WD 307 and 320 respectively) – in 1957, all three being allocated to Polmadie on 5 October. All three were officially withdrawn on 22 December 1962 and again on 3 August 1963, but both times re-instated. As seen here No 48775 is a Patricroft engine, but it moved to Lostock Hall on 6 July 1968, from where the end coincided with the demise of BR steam in August.

THE STEAM LOCOMOTIVE SHED

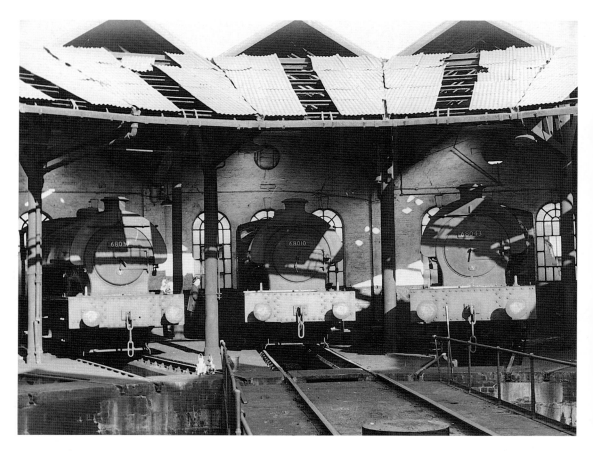

Above One would have thought that an open roundhouse would make for easier photography, but the light conditions here prove otherwise! On an unidentified date in 1964, three 'J94s' – Nos 68037, 68010 and 68043 – rest between duties at Darlington. Originally built by the NER in 1866, Darlington shed initially sported a fine conical central section. This has seen better days and, no doubt as the facility was downgraded to a stabling point for tank engines following the rebuilding of the adjacent seven-road through shed by the LNER in 1940, it has received little remedial attention. All three 'J94s' were withdrawn in May 1965. *MJS collection*

Above right In the early 1960s Fratton shed, on the outskirts of Portsmouth, was home to stored locos, including members of the National Collection. On 17 August 1963 Ray captured on film Nos 30245, 30538 and 30925 *Cheltenham*, all withdrawn within the previous 12 months. The square brick-built roundhouse (sounding like a contradiction in terms!) was opened jointly by the LB&SCR and L&SWR in 1891, and the proud possessor of two coal stages – one for each company! Wartime damage led to re-roofing in 1948, with the corrugated asbestos sheeting so beloved of the SR, and this is seen admitting the attractive shafts of sunlight.

Right Elsewhere in the shed, perhaps more glamorous fare were Nos 30850 *Lord Nelson* and 30777 *Sir Lamiel*. Note how they are here stored on short spurs from the turntable, requiring them to temporarily lose their tenders. Spending the whole period on BR's books at Eastleigh, in common with the other seven of the first eight 'Nelsons', *Lord Nelson* itself was withdrawn on 24 September 1962, whereas *Sir Lamiel* was more adventurous in its allocations, finally seeing the end at Basingstoke on 9 November 1961.

THE STEAM LOCOMOTIVE SHED

Above As if internal shed shots were not difficult enough, Ray was not afraid to also try them at night! Using flash at 1/25th second at f5.6/8, Nos 31819 and 30072 are frozen in time at Guildford on 17 November 1963, the former looking as though it has recently come in from the rain! However, it will not be sheltering between duties for much longer, being discarded from Guildford on 27 January 1964. The 'USA' tank was the more fortunate, having moved from Southampton to Guildford on 4 March 1963 and remaining in service until withdrawal with the cessation of steam on the SR in July 1967. Preservation was then to beckon on the Keighley & Worth Valley Railway.

Left As if to prove that he was committed to his art, Ray proudly records that this shot of No 76031 under repair at Guildford, alongside No 31412 in steam ready for the next duty, was taken at 3.00am on 26 February 1964! A fairly new member on Guildford's roster, No 31412 had come from Redhill on 16 September 1963, but only ran a further six months, the end coming on 17 August 1964. No 76031, new in December 1953, was similar to the 'USA' above in that it remained in action until the very end in July 1967.

THE STEAM LOCOMOTIVE SHED

Above These two shots of Guildford were also taken under conditions with that added challenge! The first, once more at night, looking inside from the open turntable, required a 10-second exposure. Engines on shed in the twilight hours of 9 March 1965 include Nos 31858, 34001 *Exeter*, 34082 *615 Squadron*, 33009, 31639, 33026, 31866, 31791 and 31873. Note that the turntable here is not in a deep pit – perhaps just as well for Ray, moving around the shed at night!

Right We are again looking into Guildford shed, but this time in daylight, and successful photography is being aggravated by driving rain! Ray merely records 16 June 1966 as being 'dull and wet', but the torrential conditions can clearly be seen against the background of the shed's interior and the smokeboxes of Nos 31405 (left) and 31791. The silhouette of No 31639's tender and cab can be seen to the right. Reflecting the run-down in the requirements for steam on the SR, none of the three captured here will move again in anger – the end for all was just 11 days away.

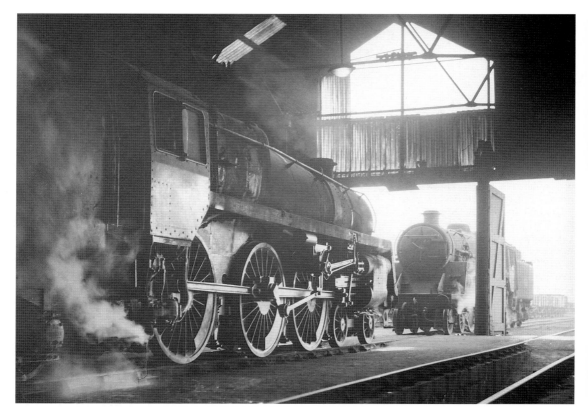

Above Ray's caption for this shot was 'Giants Resting'. 'Standard' Class 5s were hardly 'giants', but could perhaps be considered so by comparison with more diminutive types. On Sunday 18 September 1966, 'sisters' Nos 73029, with connecting rods nicely aligned, and 73022 simmer quietly at the entrance to Eastleigh's running shed before undertaking their next turns. Two more examples of wasted assets, '29 was new to Blackpool on 26 January 1952, moving to the WR in October 1953, then to the SR exactly five years later. Surviving right to the end in July 1967, its final destination was Nine Elms, from 27 June 1966. '22, meanwhile, had a similar history, after entering service at Chester on 3 November 1951. Withdrawal came slightly earlier for this loco – 15 May 1967 – but again from Nine Elms.

Below Very close to the very end of steam on the SR, Ray has once more taken up the challenge of poor light. An unidentified 'USA' tank rests inside Eastleigh on 4 June 1967, the focus of attention of a group of visiting enthusiasts. Note the absence of other locomotives, reflecting the proximity of the last days.

Right As mentioned previously, shed visits could solicit unexpected surprises and delights. Inside the roundhouse at Leeds (Neville Hill) on 26 August 1955, the photographer was pleased to record the last ex-Hull & Barnsley loco then still nominally in service. Although the brake rodding is intact, the connecting rods have gone and the dome is off, perhaps signifying that No 69114 is unlikely to work again. Coal in the bunker, however, could indicate use as a stationary boiler; withdrawal did not officially come until 17 November 1956. Built in 1894 for the NER, the shed's brick oblong containing a four-roundhouse set-up remained unaltered until BR reduced it to just two in 1960. Closure came on 12 June 1966, after which it was converted to a straight shed for diesel servicing. *Brian Morrison*

Below Still in the Leeds area, the interior of Bradford's Low Moor shed is seen on 17 September 1967, the temporary abode for Nos 61306, 44662 and 61030 *Nyala*. The presence and home allocation of these examples of different Regions betrays the shed's ambivalent career, having been controlled by both the LMR and ER. Coded 25F by the LMS in 1935 and BR in 1948, it became the ER's 56F in September 1956, then 55J in August 1967 – just one month before closure! All three of the triumvirate seen here were withdrawn with the closure, but happily No 61306 lives on, having assumed the *Mayflower* name previously gracing No 61379, withdrawn in August 1962. Long stays have been enjoyed on the Great Central and Nene Valley preserved lines. *Peter Fitton*

Above Rose Grove was similar in design to Bolton and, like its north-western neighbour, survived to the end of steam. Opened by the L&YR in 1899 as a straight six-road dead-end shed, it was re-roofed the year after Bolton, in 1947, in an identical fashion to its neighbour. Closure came with the end of BR steam in 1968. Seen in that last year, on 23 March, No 48257 peers out at yet more wet weather, while No 48491 braves the elements. The latter was withdrawn from Patricroft on 13 July 1968, while No 48257, one of Rose Grove's own, lasted until the very end. The site was subsequently subsumed under part of the M65.

Left Inside the ex-GWR shed at Shrewsbury on an unidentified date, possibly in 1957, No 5050 *Earl of St Germans* stands next to No 5004 *Llanstephan Castle*, nameplate and cab highlighted by the attractive shafts of sunlight. No 5050 emerged from Swindon in May 1936 as *Devizes Castle*, but had the personality change in August 1937; the name was subsequently used to adorn June 1946-built 'Castle' No 7002. By comparison, No 5004 was much the elder, having entered the world in June 1927. Both resided in London and the West Midlands following nationalisation and were withdrawn, respectively, on 31 August 1963 and 21 April 1962. *J. K. Morton, MJS collection*

THE STEAM LOCOMOTIVE SHED

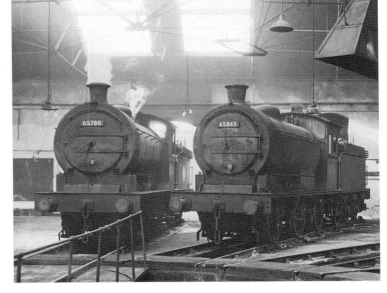

Above Stockport (Edgeley) was another shed to survive until the last days of steam on BR and is seen here on 18 November 1967, with the rudimentary blocks and curved rails used in many sheds to prevent over-running, somewhat hopefully painted white. Little altered during its life, following its opening by the LNWR on 24 May 1883, apart from a re-roofing in 1932, the eight-road depot survived until very close to the end of steam, shutting its doors on 6 May 1968. Demolition followed some time after. Left to right are Nos 48549, 44940 and 48673. The latter has probably worked its final train, being withdrawn on 2 December, while both the other '8F' and the 'Black Five' lasted until 1968 – going respectively on 13 July from Patricroft, and Stockport on 23 March.

Above right Sunderland was, for once, a large airy roundhouse, within which photographs were a relatively simple matter. Known more specifically locally as 'South Dock', this roundhouse feature was an 1875 second addition to the original NER two-road straight shed opened in 1857. Due to the 'roughly' square outside walls, it is difficult to appreciate here the slated triple-hipped roofing, seen above the lights and smoke vents. The depot closed to steam on 17 September 1967, with facilities from this section ending on that date, followed by demolition. In contrast, the original straight sheds, comprising four roads, were used as a diesel depot until the late 1980s, finally being demolished in 1990. Posing for their turn before the camera on an unidentified date in 1964 are two elderly 'J27' workhorses, Nos 65788 and 65865. The former prepares to venture out into the sun, while its neighbour is in receipt of some attention, devoid of connecting rods and with a drunken shedplate! *MJS collection*

Finally in this section, a look at a rare interloper to a location that has changed beyond recognition in more recent times. Being turned while participants of a 1964 RCTS rail tour enjoy the sights and sounds of the city, No 35007 *Aberdeen Commonwealth* presents a unique picture on the turntable of pre-National Railway Museum York roundhouse, proudly displaying its 70E Salisbury shedplate and in unfamiliar company with Nos 92006 and 62028. This was yet another Nine Elms loco that saw steam out on the SR in July 1967, while the much newer 'Standard 9F' 2-10-0 (built in January 1954) only lasted until 11 September 1965, allocated here at York. *MJS collection*

THE STEAM LOCOMOTIVE SHED

8.
GUILDFORD

Allocation in 1950: 57. Closed: 7 July 1967.

GUILDFORD.
The shed is on the west side of the line south of the station. The yard is visible from the line.

Turn right outside the station, and then first right into Farnham Road. The shed entrance is on the left hand side just past the railway under-bridge. Walking time 5 minutes.

Note.—The shed yard extends under the road bridge, and there are live rails in the vicinity of the yard.

We have already seen images of Guildford and it comes as no surprise to learn that the depot was a favourite haunt for Ray. He spent much time and expended much film there, and he delighted in using available light to best effect. Using *contre-jour*, the camera shielded by the Farnham Road overbridge, he captured the attractive lighting effects on

Nos 31408 and 31405 between the shed proper and the coal stage on 18 March 1966. Built in September 1933 and November 1932 respectively, at Ashford, they were among the last ten of Maunsell's 'N' Class two-cylinder 2-6-0s, both starting life at Ashford shed and both finishing at Guildford on the same day, 27 June 1966.

Above This most unusual view of the shed building superbly depicts the cramped situation, the open half-roundhouse chiselled into the hillside, and the steel and corrugated asbestos pitched roof fitted in 1953. Visible on shed on 27 February 1964 are Nos 75069, approaching the turntable, and 30541, fitted to a snowplough that is lost in the shadows. Interestingly, both locomotives are now preserved. The station complex is seen beyond the Farnham Road overbridge.

Left Immediately on the other side of the bridge, locos ran on to the coaling stage road. Seen here on Sunday 19 August 1962 from the vantage point of the signal gantry affixed to the bridge are Nos 33035, 33022, 33039, 33032 and 33001, with a Urie 'S15' to the left and, on the extreme right, a 2-BIL unit on a Guildford-Aldershot-Ascot-Waterloo service. Note that No 33035 is still wearing the 74D shedplate appropriate to it being allocated to Tonbridge in 1948, despite having been transferred to Guildford on 26 May 1961! It was withdrawn on 22 June 1964, the same year as the other 'Q1' 'Charlies'.

THE STEAM LOCOMOTIVE SHED

Right On 13 February 1964 Feltham-allocated 'S15' No 30836 is an unusual visitor to Guildford, more usually being seen around Redhill at this period. Built in December 1927 at Eastleigh Works, with 5 ft 7in driving wheels, and the penultimate of the first 15 'S15s', it initially did not sport the smoke deflectors, which were fitted around 1930. In 1937 it acquired the tender from 'King Arthur' No 766 *Sir Geraint* and was transferred to the Central Section of the SR. Spending some of the last war on the South Western Division, its Redhill sojourn was from 27 July 1951 to 24 June 1963, but otherwise the remainder of its BR days were spent at Feltham, ending on 22 June 1964. To the left, Guildford South signal box can just be seen and, on the right, the arm of the water pipe.

Below Fifteen days later, on 28 February, the signal box is more clearly seen as No 76032 accelerates away from the station with the 12.05pm Reading-Tonbridge passenger service, passing a Redhill-Woking freight headed by D6595. New in December 1953, to Stratford shed, No 76032 spent the first nine years of its life on the ER, transferring to the Southern on 8 December 1962, initially to Brighton, then Guildford from 16 September 1963. It had another six months of life left when seen here, being withdrawn on 17 August 1964. Note the cut-out cabside tablet-catcher.

Above left This view of the coal stage is looking south from the station footbridge, and again the generally cramped facilities at Guildford are exemplified as Nos 31790, 33001 and 34014 *Budleigh Salterton* jostle for position and attention, mid-morning on Sunday 22 March 1964. The two left-hand roads and the coal stage are the site of the original L&SWR two-road shed built in 1845. This was demolished in 1887 to accommodate station enlargements, with the later shed already seen opening to compensate. There is plenty of steam here and all, seemingly, have not a care in the world. No 33001, however, had only a further two months to go – departing current stock rosters on 25 May – while the other class leader, 'U-boat' No 31790, survived a little longer, to 8 June 1965.

Left Despite the predominance of tender locos thus far seen here, tanks were an everyday part of the Guildford diet. Viewed from across the main line south of the station, Nos 41294, 30064 and 41287 stand alongside the shed wall on 17 July 1964. No 41294 was new to the SR on 3 November 1951 and stayed with the Region throughout its life until its withdrawal on 19 September 1966, whereas its 'sister', 11 months older, first saw service at Crewe (North). Five other LMR sheds followed before a switch of territories took it to the SR on 24 June 1961 and Brighton from 6 July. A Guildford engine since 25 May 1964, it had one further move, to Eastleigh from 8 June 1965, before finally giving up the ghost on 22 August 1966.

Above The tracks between the shed and the 1887-vintage coal stage gave superb opportunities for portraits. Ex-Works and allocated to 75B (Redhill), No 30543 quietly steams by the coal stage on 27 July 1964 as the tender is replenished. Note the fast-fading chalk smiling faces on the front buffers! Built at Eastleigh in March 1939, No 30543 was a member of the SR 'Q' Class, the penultimate British 0-6-0 design, succeeded only by the 'Q1s' in 1942. It was fitted with a Bulleid chimney in April 1948, in an attempt to counter a poor front-end design and inadequate draughting, then the BR version, as seen here, in November 1961. The loco has also had a 'new' smokebox, replacing the one that previously bore a plate evidencing the position of the Maunsell snifting valves. Ostensibly built for freight, the class acquitted itself well enough on passenger turns. The end came for '43 on 21 December 1964.

The mounting evidence of locos having been cleaned of ash and clinker is threatening to provide a 'health and safety' hazard, heaped between Nos 76005 and 41294 by the coal stage on 11 August 1964. While these two receive their respective attentions, No 30833 waits in the background for its turn. The 'Standard' Class 4 2-6-0 was delivered new to Eastleigh on 8 January 1953 and stayed in the southern part of the Region for the whole of its existence. Its allocation here is Salisbury, from where it ended its days on 9 July, the last day of steam on the SR.

THE STEAM LOCOMOTIVE SHED

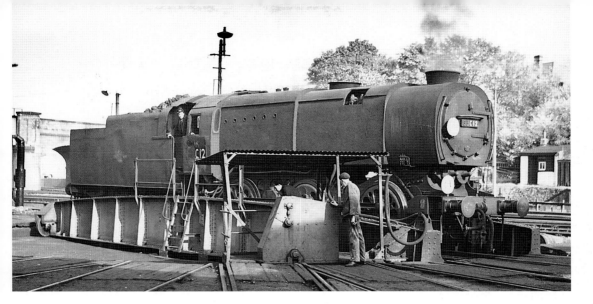

Above Humanity is prone to nostalgia and railwayman are no exception. Presumably with tongue firmly in cheek – and without official sanction? – the crew of No 33012 have attempted to turn the clock back and have inadvertently connived with Ray to recreate a pre-nationalisation scene, there being virtually nothing to betray the date. Note the unusual staff shelter on the vacuum-assisted turntable being used on 22 October 1964 to turn 'C12'. Ray knew the members of this 'Q1' Class as 'Charlies', but they also had the distinction of being 'affectionately' called 'Warthogs', 'Utilities', 'Dustbins' and even 'Spam Cans' (to some Midlands enthusiasts, although the name was more usually applied to Bulleid's unrebuilt 'Pacifics'). New in September 1942, the whole post-nationalisation period was spent at

Feltham, until transfer to Guildford just a month before this shot, on 14 September. The end was three months later, on 21 December.

Below By comparison, this portrait of 'U' Class leader No 31790 is much more humdrum, but nevertheless, posed on the line to the coal stage on 17 November 1964, it is a fine evocation of the class and its working environment. Originally built at Ashford in June 1917 as the sole SE&CR 'K' Class two-cylinder 2-6-4T, numbered A790 and named *River Avon*, it was rebuilt as a tender engine at Eastleigh in June 1928 following the Sevenoaks disaster of 24 August 1927, when No A800 *River Cray* left the road at speed. As already seen on page 98, it was withdrawn on 8 June 1965.

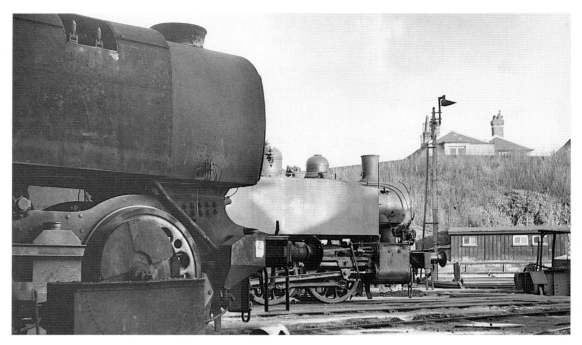

Above A comparison of locomotive design. Although both were built with utility and ease of maintenance in mind – and within a year of each other, although admittedly for wholly different classes of work – other than ease of access to working parts, the thinking on either side of the Atlantic was very different. Standing by the turntable on 3 December 1964, No 33018 (left) looks distinctly ugly compared to the slightly more graceful lines of 'USA' tank No 30072. Happily, the latter escaped cutting following withdrawal at the end of SR steam, and went on to preservation on the Keighley & Worth Valley Railway.

Below Seen from the end of the platform at Guildford station in the early morning of 3 March 1965, in a symphony of steam and, again, good use of light, 'U' Class No 31791 – of the class not altogether imaginatively known as 'U boats' – does its best not to play second fiddle to the energetic steaming of No 34051 *Winston Churchill*. The 'U' has another 15 months of life, but poor old 'Winnie' – a Salisbury resident since 1951 – was nowhere near as long-lived, going on 27 September 1965. Fortunately, the importance of the loco was recognised and preservation beckoned as part of the National Collection.

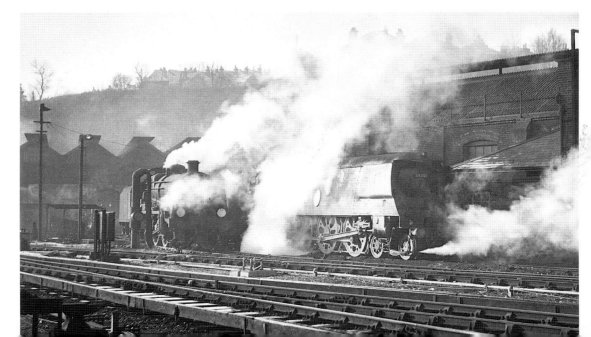

Above Seen opposite at rest, No 30072 is now at work on 12 March 1965, undertaking the shunting duties for which it was largely brought to Guildford on 4 March 1963, after spending the whole of its previous British career in and around Southampton Docks. Introduced to our railway system under the auspices of Bulleid, who wanted to replace the ageing and deteriorating Adams 'B4' 0-6-0Ts, it had been built by Vulcan Ironworks in the United States in 1943. Integrated into SR stock in April 1947, it entered Eastleigh Works in July 1948 to have its coal bunker enlarged, cab windows changed and roof ventilator fitted. Re-emerging one month later, it settled into its anonymous duties until the transfer to Guildford. Here, Driver Cummings and Fireman Alesbury take time out to pose for Ray's extensive photographic collection of the men and women he knew and worked with.

Below Undoubtedly one of the dirtiest jobs working with steam was cleaning out the smokebox. The amount of ash, dust and clinker could be prodigious, and if not cleared would certainly impair the steaming of the loco, to the distinct displeasure of driver and fireman! On Sunday 16 May 1965 two lucky young shed staff undertake the task on Nos 33027 and 33020. It is little wonder that recruiting and retaining employees for these sorts of tasks prevented the railways from having both sufficient numbers and quality of staff in the later years of the 1950s and into the 1960s. Both 'Q1's were withdrawn on the same day from Guildford – 10 January 1966.

Most photographers recognise that early morning and late afternoon/early evening light is preferable to direct, overhead midday sun for attractive effects. Using this principle to excellent effect, Ray has combined light and shade, steam and human interest to create a most pleasing view of Nos 31816, 31411 and 31866 being moved into the shed yard by a diesel shunter on 24 August 1965, while the 'gang of four' manhandle new sleepers into place alongside. Like the 'Q1s' on the last page, all three of these locos ceased work in the early months of 1966.

THE STEAM LOCOMOTIVE SHED

Above The end is nigh! Looking down on the coal stage on 6 July 1967 from the station footbridge, the depletion of steam on the SR and the proximity of its total demise is clear, compared to previous views. No 77014 is obviously in steam, but the two Bulleids look bereft of immediate life. No 34060 *25 Squadron* has lost both front number plate and nameplate, with only the support of the latter still in place, while No 34018 *Axminster* stands unattended in the background. The apparently deserted station adds to the depressing atmosphere.

Below Our old friend No 30072 is seen again, about to shunt a box wagon from the shed interior on 7 July 1967. The final loco in the shed confines at this time, it appears to be the last round-up at the roundhouse!

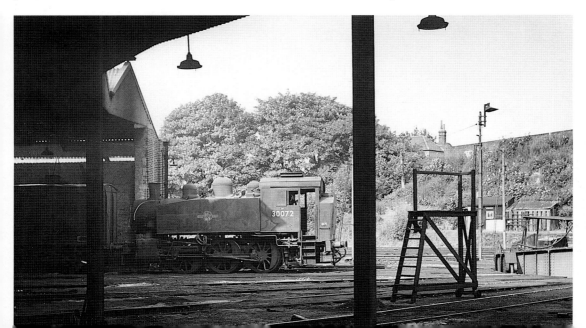

The chalked legend on the smokebox of No 76067 says it all – 'Farewell to Steam – Last of the Greats'. On 7 July 1967, the date of the formal closure of the shed, Nos 73118, once named *King Leodegrance*, and 76067 prepare for their final departure from Guildford to the open road and oblivion. Respectively built in December 1955 and August 1956, neither had reached their teenage years, nor were they to enjoy a resurrection in preservation.

THE STEAM LOCOMOTIVE SHED

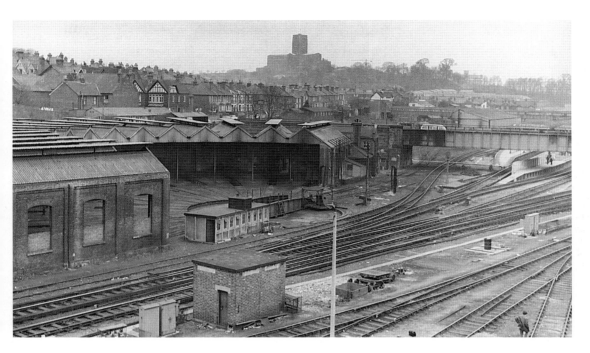

Above Less than a year after the date of the last view, the shed stands empty and forlorn. On 7 April 1968 the windows have gone and the turntable is locked into place, no more to turn mighty denizens of the steam world. Also absent is the South signal box, its site to the right of the brick-built storeroom now empty.

Below The final indignity: the water crane stands ever hopeful of being of service, but demolition of the coal stage is well under way on 8 March 1969.

9.
SCOTLAND

Although predominantly based in the south, Ray did venture north on a number of occasions and even to the furthest points of Scotland. Though not one of his photographs, he would have enjoyed views such as this, with locos totally foreign to those south of the border. On 19 June 1957 No 61994 *The Great Marquess* stands under the coaler at Eastfield shed in Glasgow. When opened in 1904, the shed was provided with a ramped coal stage, but it was replaced by the mechanical edifice seen here. Specifically built for the West Highland Line, Gresley's three-cylinder 'K4s' appeared in January 1937, not so much a brand-new design but rather a metamorphosis, with 'K3'

cylinders, 'K2' boiler and 'B17' firebox atop a chassis with 5ft 2in driving wheels. Akin to the 'K3s', they were rough-riding locos and, although being stalwarts of the route for some 15 years, were replaced in the early 1950s by Thompson's two-cylinder derivative, introduced in 1949 and designated 'K1'. The second of the original Class, *Marquess* saw birth at Darlington in July 1938, initially named *MacCailein Môr*. An Eastfield engine for many years, it moved to Dunfermline on 19 December 1959, from where it was withdrawn two years later. Happily, preservation intervened – as LNER No 3442 – on the Severn Valley Railway. *J. K. Morton, MJS collection*

THE STEAM LOCOMOTIVE SHED

With the majestic water tower edifice behind, No 44998 stands by the side of Inverness's open roundhouse on Sunday 6 August 1961, in company with Nos 44785 and D5321. The second shed site at Inverness, opened in 1863 by the Highland Railway when the original, much smaller Inverness & Nairn Railway building was subsumed into Lochgorm Works, the stone-built roundhouse was unusually graced with this grandiose structure straddling the entrance road to the shed, hiding the water tank behind the masonry. Officially closed to steam in June 1961 – despite appearances here – the depot stood to house redundant steam locos until August 1962, after which it was demolished. No 44998, like its sister 44997, was a Perth engine for the whole of its BR existence and was withdrawn on 29 April 1967. In contrast, No 44785 was an Inverness veteran until officially moved to Corkerhill on 21 April 1962; it saw its end there on 25 July 1964.

Above In another view of the scene on the previous page, now looking east across the turntable, No 44785 is here outnumbered by Sulzer and North British diesels. Two railmen pass the time of day while a fitter does the splits between Sulzer and steam just inside the shed building.

Below Looking in the opposite direction, west across the turntable, the steam engines temporarily hors de combat are obviously very shy! In addition to the five 'Black Fives', on shed on 6 August 1961 were Nos 54466, 55199, 55269, 54495, 57587 and a lone example from a totally alien parentage, ex-GWR No 1646, now stored at the shed following the closure of the Dornoch branch. This was not the end of this loco, however, as it saw further service at Perth until finally discarded on 9 February 1963.

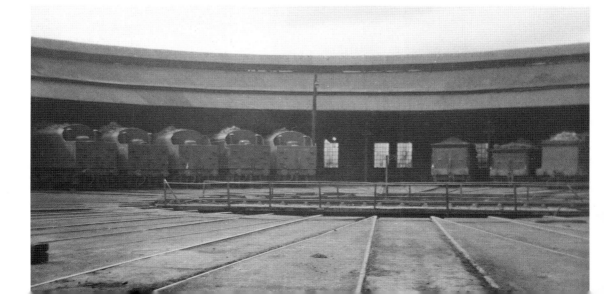

Right As we have seen before, Ray took many shots from moving trains and his trip to Scotland was no exception. His first photographic trip to the country, he did not want to pass up on chances to record locations such as Forres, seen here from an Inverness-Aberdeen diesel express, sadly deserted on Monday 7 August 1961. Built by the Inverness & Perth Railway and opened on 3 August 1863, the two-road shed was partially rebuilt by the HR in 1901. Closed in May 1959, it saw a brief reprieve as a diesel depot before the inevitable demolition.

Below Wick was not the most northerly depot in the country, but at the end of the run from Georgemas Junction (post-1944) it was the most easterly in Caithness, and one of the most isolated. On 23 August 1960 the enthusiastic visitor could be excused for feeling somewhat cheated, with a mere two locos on shed – hidden deep within – and just the antiquated crane in the yard. Note the attempt at some break from routine with the garish painted edging to the doorways and the slab of white paint on the stores building.

The two-road shed had originally opened on 28 July 1874 and stood largely unaltered until 1959, when BR saw fit to re-roof it with longitudinal smoke vents. The amendment can clearly be seen here, but one wonders whether it was economically sensible, as the depot closed to steam in July 1962 and only stored diesels for a short period. Incredibly, the building still stood at the end of the 20th century – as a supermarket! *David Johnson*

Left The phantom white doorway painter has struck again at Thurso, photographed on 11 August 1961. This was another HR depot, opened, like Wick, on 28 July 1874, this time with just one road. Closure was again in 1962 and, like Wick, the structure remained as the new Millennium dawned, this time as a carpet warehouse. Again, the visitor is to be disappointed in this 1961 view, with the shed totally devoid of motive power.

Below Steam at last! There are similarities between the shed building here at Kyle of Lochalsh and that at Wick – both built by the HR – but thankfully the white paint has not made the journey across to the Scottish west coast. Opened comparatively late, in 1897, with the extension from Strome Ferry, the depot was closed to steam on 10 June 1961 and completely one year and eight days later. Sadly, no commercial use beckoned for this structure. The atmosphere on 9 July 1957 is totally different from that at Forres and Thurso, enlivened by the presence of three locos very much in steam. No 55216 shunts some stock around the yard, while 'Black Fives' Nos 45478 and 45179 wait their call to arms. The ancient McIntosh 'Caley 439' 0-4-4T is some way from home here, being an Inverness loco since July 1952; it survived until 21 October 1961. *David Johnson*

THE STEAM LOCOMOTIVE SHED

Above Many of the Scottish sheds had long histories and architecture to match, but the facilities at Keith as seen in 1954 seem to have been renewed in the recent past, with widened entrances and steel girder supports. Indeed this is so, as BR had removed the quartet of attractive 1856-vintage stone arches over each road the previous year. The shed closed to steam in January 1961, but accommodated diesels until 1976. Partial demolition followed, with one wall being incorporated into a warehouse. Enjoying some weak sunshine in the shed yard are Nos 61539, 54482 and an unidentified 'K2'. Gresley's 'B12s' undertook much of the work from the shed during the war, only leaving in the mid-1950s; here, No 61539 has only a brief spell left, being withdrawn on 27 November 1954. No 54482 was more fortunate, working until 24 March 1962 from Aviemore. *Pat Whitehouse*

Below Back in traditional North of Scotland architectural regions, Ray is again thwarted by finding yet another deserted shed at Peterhead on 16 August 1961. Though similar in many ways to the HR sheds already seen, Peterhead was of GNofSR parentage, opening on 3 July 1862. Originally a two-road shed, only one track survives here, but, with one door to this at an unhealthy angle, it is not surprising to learn that the depot had already closed to steam – in June. Diesels used the site until 3 May 1965, after which it became another victim of 'official vandalism'!

Above Ray was a little luckier in his visit to Scotland two years later, and found three diesels present on Oban shed on Sunday 25 May 1963. They are frustratingly hidden away in the shed, however, and he was forced to capture the remaining items of rolling-stock and infrastructure, of which the unusual mechanical coaling plant and turntable were 'hors de combat'. Already closed 19 days previously, all this provision is living on borrowed time.

Below Boat of Garten was but a few miles north of Aviemore, but the presence of an engine shed there was due to its GNofSR roots. On 11 July 1957 No 78054 has plenty of boiler pressure ready for its next turn, while elsewhere all is quiet, with No 57634 well inside the shed and *Ben Alder* unceremoniously parked at the end of the siding on the right. The latter was stored here until 1961, pending preservation, although sadly that was not to be. The depot officially closed in November 1958 and was demolished after *Ben Alder* left. No 78054 – new on Christmas Eve 1955 to Motherwell – was a Keith engine when seen here. Subsequent homes were Aberdeen (Ferryhill) and Bathgate, from where withdrawal came on Christmas Day 1965 – having just managed to reach its tenth birthday. *David Johnson*

Perhaps not surprisingly, Fort William was a much better prospect for Ray, and his visit in 1963 was not to disappoint, despite the shed having been closed to steam since 18 June 1962. Of West Highland Railway conception, the depot opened on 7 August 1894, a brick-built through shed, with a gable-style slate roof. After closure to steam, it gave succour to diesels for roughly a decade. On 31 May 1963 two 'J37s' are unusually present, with Nos 64592 and 64636 especially brought to the shed and caringly buffed up for working a SLS special trip to Mallaig.

Above Elsewhere, tucked away behind Fort William's shed on 31 May 1963 was No 44255, in store but complete with self-weighing tender and accompanied by the depot snowplough and an 08 diesel shunter with a rake of waste wagons. Having been a resident of St Rollox shed from nationalisation until 18 January 1958, No 44255 then moved to Fort William, from where it was withdrawn four months prior to this view, on 19 January 1963.

Below Steam still hung on in Scotland in 1963, but the mainstay of workings to Fort William were the Sulzer Type 2 diesels, with D5351 and D5356 present on 31 May. Note the cab cut-outs for the tablet-catchers. The turntable, standing on the southern edge of the shed yard, dated from the opening of the shed in 1894.

The sheds of the Ayrshire area had a wholly different feel from those already seen, being the result of G&SWR thinking. A six-road dead-end shed, Hurlford opened in 1877, complete with attractive cathedral-style windows in the gable ends; closure came just short of 90 years later, on 6 October 1966. Presenting a delightful picture on shed in the bright sunshine of 1 September 1957 are Nos 56368, 57577, 77017 and 57622.

The two McIntosh 'Caley 812s' lasted until September 1962, although only No 57577 was then still a Hurlford engine, whereas ex-'29' Class No 56368 succumbed on 30 December 1961, a Hurlford loco the whole of its BR life. Note the rudimentary lifting tackle above the right-hand doorway, and how the 'health and safety' white paint has been much more tastefully applied here! *J. K. Morton, MJS collection*

Below Ayr shed was another to share the G&SWR 'cathedral' architectural style. With an allocation in 1950 of 59, it was a satisfying place to visit and even towards the end of steam in the area was home to variety. The second of two sites in Ayr, the G&SWR built a six-road twin-gabled depot in 1879. In 1959 the westernmost half – to the right here – was extended at both ends to accommodate the insurgence of DMUs. Thereafter steam occupied the remaining three roads, until closure to steam on 3 October 1963 – this section was demolished in the 1970s. On 7 June 1963 No 44977 quietly steams at the entrance to the 'holy place', next to the tender of a MR '4F'. The 'Black Five' had been an Ayr loco since 8 September the previous year and soldiered on until 31 December 1966. Note its large 'St Rollox'-style cabside numbers.

Below St Rollox was also an exciting place to visit, being next to the Works of the same name and often home to locos either entering or leaving the Works premises. The 12-road shed opened in 1916, replacing the previous four-road affair that stood in the yard of the Works. No amendments or alterations were made during its existence and closure came on 7 November 1966. Perhaps surprisingly, the ramped coaling stage was not part of the shed yard, but rather a separate wooden facility next to the main running line. On 19 May 1964 No 45471 looks as though it might have seen some attention at the Works, being very smart compared to 'sister' No 45473. *Tom Heavyside*

Above Another view of a shed yard from a train was obtained at Perth, photographed from the 9.25am Crewe-Perth express on 19 June 1965. LMR and ER passenger locos rub shoulders before setting off for widely differing destinations, while three small diesel shunters wait for the next duty. 'A2/3' No 60512 *Steady Aim* is the only loco identifiable and, being a Polmadie loco at this date, has presumably worked in from Glasgow. One week after this shot it was nominally transferred to Dundee (Tay Bridge) shed and immediately withdrawn! The three shunters look to be Barclay 0-4-0s (later BR Class 06) – Perth had an allocation of D2411, D2412 and D2444 at this time.

Below Photographed from 'The Grampian' express, hauled by No 60009 *Union of South Africa* nearing its destination at Aberdeen, is Ferryhill shed yard. The 10-road shed is here seen under its 1949 re-slated roof, with an EE Type 4 (later Class 40) preparing to leave. The young spotters enjoying the bright sunshine of 22 June 1965 are obviously tolerated, sitting on the bridge parapet, no doubt keen to record the numbers of what Ray noted as being 'A4s, WD, LMS 5, diesel Type 4 and "350" shunter'. The shed closed to steam on 18 March 1967, and totally on 6 December 1987.

Returning south, Ray is again passing Perth shed yard, one week after the last view, aboard the 8.20am Inverness-Edinburgh express of 26 June 1965. The quantity and quality of locomotives appear to have improved over the ensuing seven days, and Ray noted 'A1', 'Black Five', 'Britannia', 'Standard' '9F' and Type 4 and 2 diesels. Opened by the CR in 1854, the seven-road shed survived, with some modifications, until 1937, after which a new LMS-built eight-road shed replaced it immediately to the south, known as 'Perth South' in BR days. This latter opened on 14 May 1938, with 'all mod cons' of the time. Closure to steam was on 14 May 1967 – 39 years to the day from opening! – and total closure came two years later, on 5 October 1969. The extensive building was demolished in 1972.

       THE STEAM LOCOMOTIVE SHED

One further visit was made north of the border in 1991. Obviously there was no steam by this time, but at least it provided Ray with a chance to record an old steam depot new to him. Converted for use by the engineer's department, and obviously in good state, Crianlarich is pictured on 15 July 1991. The facility was opened by the West Highland Railway on 7 August 1894, but was an early casualty, being closed by the LNER in 1930. Obviously well cared for in this view, it was still standing at the end of the 20th century.

10.
TURNTABLES

What goes around, comes around! On 3 March 1961 the engineman pauses from his exertions with the table handle to allow the photographer the pleasure of recording this delightful portrait of unrebuilt 'Patriot' No 45537 *Private E Sykes V.C.* at the rear of Leicester (Midland) shed's yard. Though not rare at this location, these locos were never common here, except for a regular pick-up goods working to Nuneaton during this period. Built in July 1933 at Crewe, from the 'skeleton' of 'Claughton' No 6015, and first allocated the 5537 number on 25 June 1934, it assumed its BR persona on 8 May 1948. Its first home was Longsight and it was withdrawn on 16 June 1962, with 1,304,901 miles on the clock. It is here mated with tender 3899, originally attached to a 'Royal Scot' and acquired on 4 March 1960 during a Heavy General repair at Crewe. The 60-foot turntable was installed when the LMS completely rebuilt the shed layout at Leicester in 1945. *Alec Swain, MJS collection*

THE STEAM LOCOMOTIVE SHED

Above Turning tables by hand was no easy task, especially with large express locos, although five men to carry out the job with a MR '2P' is perhaps a little excessive; apparently the crew were having problems with the turntable's vacuum engine! During Grand National Day, 25 March 1961, No 40684, unlined and still with the original BR 'lion and wheel' emblem, is being turned at the ex-L&YR Aintree depot, having worked in as pilot to No 45534 *E. Tootal Broadhurst* from Wigan on a special from Euston. This was the 1937 site of the table, replacing the original 50-foot facility of 1886. When seen here, No 40684 had been a Bank Hall loco since 8 August 1953, but would not have this sort of attention for much longer, being withdrawn on 15 July. *Peter Fitton*

Below Presumably the engine problem had been fixed by the following year; certainly fewer hands seem to be succeeding with No 46146 *The Rifle Brigade* on Aintree's table on 31 March 1962. Built in October 1927, looking very much a cousin to the SR's 'Lord Nelsons' with rear-sloping firebox and massive smokebox, No 46146 carried the name *Jenny Lind* until the mid-1930s. Rebuilt when 16 years old, in October 1943, to the taper-boiler style seen here, the 'Royal Scot' emerged into BR's care in 1948 at Crewe (North), then spending its career between 17 July 1951 and withdrawal on 1 December 1962 oscillating between London and Carlisle depots. *Peter Fitton*

Although internally roundhouses were just that – round – externally most were not, as seen here at Hasland. Accommodating a round layout and central turntable within a square building, the shed was constructed on the east side of the main line, south of Chesterfield station, in 1875. Originally with a triple-pitched gable-style slated roof, this was replaced in later years by corrugated iron sheeting (which must had made a wonderful noise in heavy rain!). Due to the nature of the mining area in which it was located, subsidence caused problems over the years, until BR became sufficiently concerned about the fabric of the building to remove part of the roof, as seen in this view on 31 March 1962. It is perhaps fortunate, therefore, that the sun is shining on Nos 44603, 44288, 90714 and the rest of the workaday, unglamorous locos. Of the three identified locos, the two '4F's saw withdrawal in 1964, at Hasland, whereas the 'Austerity' ended its day at Frodingham on 9 January 1965. *MJS collection*

THE STEAM LOCOMOTIVE SHED

Above Those of us around at the time well remember the harsh winter of 1962/3. The snow began on Boxing Day and seemingly did not stop until the latter part of February! On 8 January 1963 there is already a widespread covering on both town and railway at Redhill as No 31627 provides some antidote to the cold, while its poor fireman gallantly pushes the table to the required position, having arrived on a passenger working from Reading. Originally blessed with a 45-foot table in a different part of the yard, Redhill gained this 65-foot version in 1928. The 'U-boat' was a Guildford loco for the whole of its BR life, ending work on 25 October 1965.

Right Designs of turntable were not wholly standardised, but the type with supporting struts seen on this 65-foot example at Reading (South) provided by the SR (and Redhill above) were not common. On 4 March 1964 driver George Powell grins (grimaces?) as he turns his charge, 'Standard' 2-6-4T No 80140, before working back to Redhill. A Class 'N' and a 'Charlie' ('Q1') wait at the side of the shed. New in July 1956 to New England, No 80140 decamped to the SR in December 1959, working from Tunbridge Wells West from the 31st. Subsequently visiting Brighton, it moved on to Redhill on 6 January 1964 (note the 75B shedplate worn here), Feltham on 8 June 1965, and finally Nine Elms on 17 October 1966. It was withdrawn from there at the very end of steam on the SR.

Above On 20 April 1965 ex-SR fireman Jack Stringer is far from home at Spa Dyke, Blackpool Central, as he walks towards the front of No 44905, watched by his driver from the cab. Built at Crewe at the end of 1945, the 'Black Five' was a long-time stalwart of Barrow-in-Furness shed, but from 1959 spent its days switching between Edge Hill (Liverpool) and Carnforth, from where it finished work on 2 December 1967. Peter Fitton

Below Many turntables were short affairs – some only able to handle tank engines – a legacy of history in most cases. An example of a 50-foot facility was at Highbridge, latterly at the end of the ex-Somerset & Dorset branch from Evercreech Junction. Although the depot was closed on 11 May 1959, facilities continued in occasional use, as seen here on 5 March 1966, the last day of the S&D. A Templecombe loco at the time, No 41249 has worked in on an enthusiasts' special and is being turned ready for the return trip. Its life will not be long hereafter, however, as withdrawal came on 27 March.

THE STEAM LOCOMOTIVE SHED

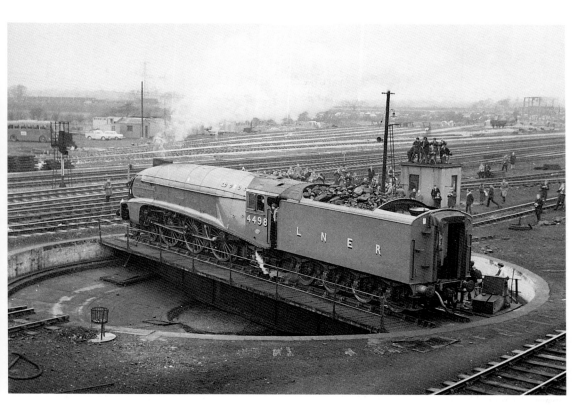

A fitting finale. Thankfully, many steam locos have escaped the cutter's torch, some to be reborn into active service. One of the very earliest, even before the end of steam on BR, was No 4498 (ex-60007) *Sir Nigel Gresley*. Built in November 1937 – the 100th Gresley-designed 'Pacific' – and withdrawn from active service from Aberdeen (Ferryhill) on 26 March 1966, the loco was happily saved from an ignominious end by the A4 Locomotive Society Ltd. On 1 April 1967 it made its inaugural run in preservation from Crewe to Carlisle and is seen here turning on Kingmoor's facility, at the southern end of the yard, watched by the 'ants' running and climbing on to every available vantage point. The sheds may have closed, but steam lives on!

INDEX OF LOCATIONS